The

HOLISTIC ROAD
To Healthy Relationships

The
HOLISTIC ROAD
To Healthy Relationships

A holistic approach for being happy and
living with other people

ANTHONY CHADWELL

authorHOUSE®

AuthorHouse™
1663 Liberty Drive
Bloomington, IN 47403
www.authorhouse.com
Phone: 1-800-839-8640

Cover Credits: Jeanette Lloyd-Stern

Published by AuthorHouse   10/26/2012

ISBN: 978-1-4772-8224-3 (sc)
ISBN: 978-1-4772-8225-0 (e)

Library of Congress Control Number: 2012919504

This Book is Dedicated

To my mother, Eileen, who emphasized the importance of reading and endured my struggle to grow up; to my wife, Marsha, who provided continuous support and encouragement during the writing of this book; and to my two children, Allisha and Blake, who gave me a reason to keep trying.

Acknowledgements

To Gloria Taylor-Brown, for her insights, which set the ball in motion in Southern California; to Ariela Wilcox, for the "kick in the pants" to get started, and for her initial guidance on structure and timelines; to Wendy Warren-Brooks, for her magnificent help with editing and formatting; to Jeanette Lloyd-Stern for the great graphics on the cover and to Cindy Mishlove, for helping with clarity and consistency.

Disclaimer

Nothing printed or reproduced from this writing is intended to diagnose, treat, prescribe or cure any physical or mental problem or medical condition and is intended for educational purposes only. The statements in this writing have not been evaluated by the FDA, and as such, shall not be construed as medical advice, implied or otherwise. The reader is advised they have sole responsibility for all of their health care decisions.

Contents

Introduction

My desire for this book is to provide a way for people to have better and more balanced relationships. The examples and solutions come from real life.

I chose the topic of relationships, because that is where people experience the most emotional pain. My hope is to give you, the reader, a practical set of tools that can be applied to any relationship. This book contains the typical examples I see most frequently. Perhaps you will relate to at least some of these examples.

Relationships are as complex and varied as the people who participate in them. No one book or, for that matter, series of books, can answer all the possible questions that pertain to interacting with other people. My hope is that you will use this book as a "quick guide" to identify your problem area and immediately have a method you can use to improve your situation.

In the clinic, I have developed a way to naturally work from a deeply intuitive place. When I work with an individual, I have developed the ability to instinctively draw specific beneficial information from the person in front of me. This ability is not easy to duplicate outside of a clinical one-on-one environment. A challenge in writing a book is to provide counsel that can be applied to more than just one person, for a wider group of people. To solve this concern, I have adapted general information that will assist this larger group of people by way of sharing "case studies," common scenarios that will resonate with readers.

I am not excepted from the stress and pain caused by relationships. I have applied many of these ideas to my own life with great benefit. My personal belief is that no one should teach something he has not thoroughly learned himself. I can honestly say that, at least for now, the major relationships in my life are happy, balanced, and beneficial for everyone involved.

It has not always been that way!

I was born in a small town in the rural West. I was born to a young, unmarried mother. This fact did not please my conservative Protestant grandparents who helped raise me. This unbalanced family arrangement created an environment of emotional tension. I certainly felt loved, but even as a young child, I did not feel safe. I had a deep pain in my heart, a strange feeling of impending doom.

My mother eventually married a man who had his own issues. After they were married, we moved to a large city, and I was forced to leave my grandparents. Because my grandparents were a huge part of my life and sense of security, I was terrified. I remember writing "I won't go" on a bunch of scraps of paper and placing them all over the house. I guess it was my 6-year-old form of rebellion.

As a grown man, I feel a little silly telling this story from my childhood. I want to minimize the emotion of it, but it is "my story," and I need to be honest about what happened to me, because that is what affected me and caused me to react to future relationships in predictable ways. Also, if *I* can be honest, at some level it gives *you*, my reader, permission to be honest, as well.

As I look back, I realize that my stepfather was very likely an alcoholic. There were many times he came home so sick from drinking that I could hear him vomiting. One day he abruptly stopped drinking alcohol without any treatment. Strangely, he started drinking Coke, a lot of Coke, like, a case a day. At the time, of course, I did not know anything about trading one addiction for another.

I was also aware of the strange relationship he had with my mother. He usually slept in the reclining chair in the living room, while she slept in the bedroom. I had grown so accustomed to this that I did not realize it was unusual until my friends would ask me about it.

Later in life, I learned from my mother that he had experienced some type of abuse as an altar boy in the Catholic church. Looking back, I see how he must have tried to deal with the trauma he had experienced by first using alcohol and then using sugar, in the form of soda, as a way to change his mood.

Another habit he had, and one I adopted myself, was over-working. In my household a "man's value" was derived from how hard and how well he worked. Being in a blue-collar home, this meant hard physical work.

My stepfather would work 60-70 hours a week. I quickly learned that when I worked hard, I got a lot of good things. First, I received positive reinforcement in the form of praise, and second, I earned money that allowed me to have fun. Money became a major motivator in my twenties and thirties.

Having started life under less than ideal circumstances, I am keenly aware of how my environment affected my reality—for better or worse. I do not observe this with any self-pity or blame. Life just is what is—it's "messy," and we all have a story. This is especially true as a child, when the ability to understand the situation you are in is matched only by your inability to do anything about it. As a child I remember feeling locked in my familial circumstances and was frustrated by my inability to do anything to change them.

The environment in which I grew up was full of mistrust and unspoken anger. It was also filled with unhealthy emotional triangles between the three of us: my mother, stepfather, and myself. I kept my stepfather's secrets from my mother, and I kept my mother's secrets from my stepfather. Secrets are a poison to the body. That poison started showing up in me.

I developed into a sensitive kid and learned quickly to anticipate other people's moods, to change my personality and actions to accommodate them. This chameleon-like behavior was very useful to minimize stress in the family but left me fearful and anxious. The emotional pressure I felt caused abdominal pain, and eventually ulcers. This was probably my first experience with what would later be called somatic-emotional response to stress.

I was fortunate; I never suffered from the very serious childhood traumas that some people experience. There was no physical or sexual abuse or neglect, yet my early environment did create a strong need in me to escape my feelings.

This fear and anxiety, along with my genetic predisposition to alcoholism, set me up to use substances as a way to cope with these feelings. For anyone who has the genetic wiring for addiction, it is only a matter of time until the addiction develops and takes priority over all other areas in your life. What starts out as a lot of fun soon becomes fun mixed with some trouble. Eventually it progresses to just trouble!

This downward spiral for me progressed until I was drinking every chance I got. I also began to suffer the consequences of so much alcohol intake. Hangovers were becoming a daily ritual.

At a very conscious level, I thought that getting married would be the solution I needed to stop using so much alcohol.

I married at 24 and quickly had two children of my own. If one comes from a home filled with dysfunction and stress, without conscious effort to counteract this, one automatically recreates dysfunction and stress in one's own family later. This was obvious from the over-materialistic priorities I had in my life. My early environment did not teach me much in the way of effective problem-solving. My wife and I bickered constantly. I over-worked much of the time, which eventually led to severe migraine headaches.

In a half-hearted effort, I tried seeking relief from the headaches from several medical doctors. I had good insurance and saw many specialists. As is typical, their answer was some kind of pill. If you are an alcoholic and take pain pills, guess what happens? That's right, you get addicted to both!

Addiction continued to be a major problem for me for almost 15 years. It was only with help from extraordinary people, and my underlying faith in God, that I was ultimately able to recover.

One of the things that helped me recover was finding a practitioner who helped me detoxify my physical body. I was a toxic mess! I looked much older than I was. My eyes had turned to an ugly brown. They are a clear blue hazel now. My organs were full of poison, and that toxicity created, in turn, toxic, confused thoughts that led to more bad behavior.

I had developed a chronic pain pattern in my upper back, neck, and head. Part of the problem stemmed from a rollover car accident I'd had when I was 17—thanks, again, to alcohol. The other part of the physical pain was a lack of appropriate curves in my spine. This had simply been part of my development. When your spine is out of alignment, nothing in your body works as well as it should.

I needed to have some serious structural alignment and integration to free up my body and reduce the pain. In an effort to get some relief, I started looking into various types of manual treatments. I tried chiropractic, massage, Rolfing, and oriental medicine. It was not until an osteopath in Canada treated me that I found any consistent relief for my physical pain. (This, in part, explains why I spent so many years learning how to provide this beneficial osteopathic treatment to others.) It was a real eye opener to see how my lifestyle had affected every part of my body, even my skeletal system.

Changing my diet and adding appropriate nutritional supplements also helped tremendously. Another wonderful practitioner was kind enough to help me discover exactly what foods and additional nutrients were right for me. My energy soared, my thoughts calmed down, and most important, my cravings for drugs and alcohol subsided!

As my body calmed down, I could see even more acutely that my life was out of balance. I had no real plan. I had nothing bigger than myself as a reference point in the world. I always believed in "God," but now, finding out what that really meant took on a new urgency. I started to explore different churches and religions. I read about different spiritual systems and beliefs. I investigated 12-step programs.

I also started doing yoga again. I first experienced yoga at the age of fourteen, from the only lady in our city who taught yoga, in 1974. It was great and planted a "seed" for my spiritual life. It was hard to believe that 20 years had passed before I reinitiated that wonderful spiritual practice for myself. *Yoga, combined with meditation, proved to be essential for me to live a balanced and chemically free life.*

Only by having been in the "trenches," am I really able to understand and help others, when they are in their "dark times." There is an empathy that comes from having been in similar pain, that is an important part of being a health care practitioner. People know they can trust you, because you have been there. This also provides hope, because they have proof that someone can be in a desperate situation and return to a balanced life of health and of helping others.

The outcome of my own, and others' similar situations, is predictable. If relationships and environment are stressful, everyone will act out in some way to find comfort. This acting out may be in minor ways like excessive hobbies, sports, and television, or more destructive ways like substance abuse and sexual promiscuity.

As these escapist habits get entrenched over time, they can lead to difficulties with all of our relationships and our interaction with the world in general. By not learning how to have healthy, balanced relationships, we may go to extremes.

We may be unable to have deep and honest relationships, because we cannot "be still" long enough to experience the good in life. The compulsive urge for the excitement that is found, especially in the early stages of dating and sex, may be so strong that being with one person for any length of time seems boring.

The opposite may also be true. Since we have experienced such turbulence in prior relationship environments, finding someone who provides even a brief or occasional escape from that stress, or some financial security, may give us a reason to stay despite obvious problems in other areas.

These are only two of many common patterns people develop as they try to get comfortably "inside their own skin." There are many others. If one talks to enough people over time, one can see the various patterns that develop.

This book can serve as a quick guide to figuring out what is going wrong and why. It may also quickly help you find a way to improve your situation.

Having been in the holistic health field for so long, with that unique eye into human behavior patterns, I have learned one thing above all others: relationship frustration causes more pain than any other problem.

My desire to help more people more quickly with practical suggestions that work, is one of the reasons I have written this book. Another reason is that writing helps to categorize the various solutions that have I developed over the last 15 years into what I now call the Chadwell Method™.

Let me give you an example. I have met with people who have done traditional talk therapy with counselors for years with only limited success. I am not saying that this type of therapy is without value, because it does have benefits. The issue I find is that no matter how many times you "talk" over a problem, it does not necessarily mean you will improve.

There have been many times when I have asked someone a question, and he begins to cry. When I ask what is going on, he will often answer with frustration, "I thought I worked through all of that," or, "I have been working on that for years; I thought it was gone."

Here is what I discovered: if the basis of the problem is not emotional, in my opinion, talk therapy is of limited value.

Here are some more examples. If your hormones are out of balance, you must correct that *first*, so that you can have consistent moods with which to make decisions on a day-to-day basis.

Also, if your digestion is off and is thus affecting your mood, creating pain, or causing a negative self-image, this becomes primary and needs to be resolved before major emotional clearing can take place. Many neurotransmitters that the brain uses to function are created in the digestive tract. Bringing health to the digestive system changes brain chemistry for the better.

Finally, when you know that what you are going through right now is a spiritual lesson that you must learn, like forgiveness, you need to be supported in a way that allows you to make that connection. You need to be aware that you can never permanently solve the real, underlying problems, until you take all of these aspects into account and focus treatment in the correct area.

A person desiring to bring about change needs to look at all facets of a person's life before creating a solution. This seems so obvious to me, but I was amazed to learn that no one around me was doing it! Here are some common illustrations.

- If the problem is physical, at the very least, one needs to look at structure and emotion.
- If the problem is digestion, one needs to look at diet and exercise.
- If the problem is mood, one needs to look at hormones, diet, and the client's spiritual life.
- If the problem is with relationship, one needs to look at everything!

The Chadwell Method came out of this awareness. After a very thorough exploratory consultation, I've learned to quickly assess someone, find the root cause of the problem(s), and suggest a starting point for that person. This helps them feel better immediately. As a coach who provides guidance and encouragement, my hope is that this book will do the same thing for you right now, while you are frustrated and confused: suggest a starting point for what to do and how to change.

The chapters that follow will outline the most common relationship problems I have observed. You will immediately be drawn to one or more of the chapter headings. Go ahead and read those first. After you read those, please go back and read the rest of the chapters. Life is complex and does not fit easily into nice, neat chapters, though some chapters in this book will likely resonate with you more than others. If you currently do not relate to one of them, read it anyway. You may need the information in the future, or you may need it to be able to help someone you care about.

Each chapter is divided into four sections that help you identify the characteristics of a particular pattern. The first section will help you identify if this pattern is operating in your life. Stories from real situations have been used throughout the book to provide examples that people can relate to. Obviously, names and details have been changed to maintain anonymity. The second section will help you see how this pattern may have developed. The third section will give you practical suggestions to help you improve your life. The fourth section is a brief, bulleted outline of the solutions. This portion can be used as a quick reminder of what to do to make change now!

Anyone who reads this book will find at least some useful suggestions about dealing with various aspects of your relationships. Resolving these problems will lead to a happier and more contented life. So keep an open mind and a willing heart and let's get started!

Chapter 1:

The Chadwell Method™

"Always be willing to abandon what you know when presented with evidence of something better."—Anthony Chadwell

As I first became interested in the concept of holistic health and began researching it, I was amazed at the diversity of treatment options. Massage, chiropractic, acupuncture, exercise, nutrition, meditation, prayer, and osteopathy are just a few that have yielded significant benefits for millions of people.

My first area of learning was iridology, the study of the colored ring in the eye. It was amazing to find that the patterns in that small area of the body actually help identify problems people are having. With this information, I was able to start pinpointing areas in a person's body or her life that needed improvement. After a few months of study, I started to learn what herbs can be used to speed the process of improvement. All in all, my study of iridology and my application of it in my early practice provided a good experience. However, some results were often frustrating because there would be those clients who would not follow through with the recommended plan, or they simply would not come back for another evaluation.

At that time, I had no idea of the many complex issues that prevent or stop a person from taking the actions necessary to improve his life. This phenomenon would happen even after the client would seek me out, come in, ask for help, verbally commit to the necessary follow-through for my advice to yield benefit, and, of course, then *pay* for the advice!

I figured I must just need more education, so I spent the next 8 years studying anatomy, doing cadaver dissections, and learning many different techniques and styles of hands-on therapy and bodywork. The yield of this was great! Many people did respond, improve, and actually came back for more treatments.

I found that most people *like* to have a practitioner work on them, and to make them the focus of attention for an hour. The problem was that no matter what technique I used, a certain percentage of people would come back week after week with the same issue. Hindsight being the great teacher, I am glad they did as it allowed me to gain more skill, but it was still frustrating to have such mixed results when I knew that better success was achievable if only the client would follow the actions advised.

I began reading a lot of old books about osteopathy, chiropractic, and various other forms of naturopathic health. These books told about successes, time after time. They all seemed to be treating a different type of person than was coming to my offices, one who was able to recover quickly after just a few treatments.

I assumed again that I needed more education. My next steps were to begin studying how nutrition affects the body—not just recent information, but how nutritionists and doctors applied the science 50 or even 100 years ago. It became evident to me that the foods we are eating today are not grown or processed in the same way as they were back then. I was researching this information in the late '90s, even before genetically-modified foods and irradiation processes were as common as they are today. As a result of what I learned about soil depletion, and how the essential nutritional components are lost during processing, I added a lot of nutritional products to my repertoire.

Amazing things began to happen. People started to get *much* better. They came back more regularly, they appreciated the improvement, and they even started referring other people to my clinic.

This was a great "ah-hah moment" for me in my practice, since a higher percentage of people were getting better. I felt good about the successes, but I was still conscious of a gnawing feeling that I had yet more to learn.

Cranial-Sacral Therapy

Through an interesting series of events, I was introduced to the concepts of cranial-sacral therapy, and later, to osteopathic cranial work. The benefits of these disciplines, applied to myself, were nothing short of miraculous.

When I was 17 years old, I was involved in a very serious rollover car accident. I was taken to the hospital, was told "nothing was broken," and I would be fine in a few days. In a way I was fine: I did not look injured, and I was able to return to school. What I did not realize was that my ability to do mathematics had been severely diminished! I also started feeling depressed and exhibiting other unhealthy behaviors.

By the time I got to college, any class that involved math was too difficult, despite the fact that I had tested very high in that academic area just a few years earlier. I had no idea why math had become so frustrating. I did the best I could, but I eventually dropped out of university after the second year.

It was almost 20 years later that I began to find the answer to the changes in my ability to "do math." My first cranial session lasted over an hour. To the neophyte (which I was at the time), a cranial session can seem very "inconsequential." It is a very relaxing and, one could say, "noninvasive" modality. Afterward I felt some nausea and light-headedness. I could not believe that a treatment, which outwardly seemed so minimal, could have such a strong effect on me. As I was driving home I suddenly felt as if a piece of cellophane was literally being pulled off of my brain. Within a day or two I felt unusually calm and centered. I had a few more treatments. Each seemed to build upon the last session. Within a year I returned to college and was eventually able to pass classes in calculus and trigonometry.

The effect was so bliss-like and beneficial that I quickly started learning everything I could about the history and application of this form of treatment. Even more fascinating, I found that the principles of cranial therapy can be applied with advantage to any area of the body, not just the head.

After 2 years of study/application, I felt confident enough to add this treatment modality into my day-to-day practice. Time and time again I've seen how emotional, physical, and generational trauma gets "locked" into the body, and how this gentle and precise way of treating the body helps "unlock" that energy, so one can live and feel better.

Over the years of my practice, I have had many poignant cases of people who came to see me, and whom I chose to treat with cranial work. I will share one now.

Julie

Julie came to visit me at the suggestion of a friend. She had been having migraine headaches for years and had seen all kinds of specialists. Julie had also taken several different drugs seeking relief. Some of them had helped for a while, but the painful headaches always returned. The ineffective help and the aggravating side effects frustrated her. She had recently stopped taking a strong narcotic because it caused constipation. When she stopped taking the drug, according to her doctor's advice, she went into a kind of withdrawal and was miserable for a week. She described that time as "living hell."

She broke down in tears as she told me that the doctor's latest suggestion was that she have a total hysterectomy, "because her problem was probably hormonal!" Naturally, this recommendation came as a real shock to her, as she was only 26 at the time, and the thought of not being able to have children was unbearable to her.

As Julie sat across the desk from me I could see that one eye was lower than the other. The ear on one side of her head was also lower than the one on the opposite side. The skin on the low side had a different texture and color than the skin on the other side of her face.

I asked Julie if she had ever had any major head trauma. She recounted several bumps she had experienced. None of these were very severe, but the cumulative impact of these injuries could have been significant. After only our first cranial therapy session, she felt an improvement. When she came back for her second session, she told me she had "remembered" something her mother had once told her: when she was four years old, the entire family had been in a major vehicle accident. Julie had suffered a blow to her head on the window—the same side as her lower eye and ear.

I noted with interest that Julie had not "remembered" this incident until after the first cranial treatment. It may be that there was no reason to remember the accident until the body had a way to resolve it. After 5 or 6 sessions her headaches went away, and perhaps even more importantly, she was treated noninvasively through gentle maneuverings, and she still has her reproductive organs.

I was amazed at how obvious this problem was, when observed from a structural standpoint, and even more amazed that no one else had considered this as a possible cause.

Upon reflection I realized that most doctors and practitioners only focus on one area. The old adage, "if all you own is a hammer everything looks like a nail," is very true. This is due in part to the education system that breaks down complicated ideas, like the human body is, into manageable parts. This is fine, but then no one ever puts it all back together again. Perhaps this is why we have so many specialties and sub-specialties like dermatology, cardiology, and even pediatric urology. People become expert in one area and refer problems outside of their scope of practice to other specialists.

No one seems to be in a great position to take the necessary time to look at all aspects of the patient. And it's all complicated even further by insurance reimbursement procedures and the short visit time that's become common in the medical world. We tend to treat the symptoms but miss the root causes.

As I alluded, a significant part of this story is that Julie could not "remember" the car accident until after her first treatment. I have found this to be a very common experience among my Cranial Sacral clients. I believe the body very graciously holds our trauma for us. Not until it is appropriate, and the necessary resources are available to bring about the healing, is it necessary to become fully aware of the prior circumstances. This is a kindness the body does for us, sort of a body intelligence if you will. If we remembered *all* of our traumas at one time with no way to resolve them, we would be too overwhelmed.

Another hurdle to healing is that many people will not consider treatment solutions that do not have "scientific" proof. Science has brought about many wonderful improvements in life, but not everything can be seen under a microscope. For example, no one has ever *seen* a thought, yet we all have them. Likewise, we can't really see wind in the air. We can see effects of the wind—leaves blowing, flags fluttering, and such—but we cannot actually see *wind* itself. To say that thoughts don't exist would be ridiculous, even though we cannot see or touch or taste or smell them. And in truth no one knows for sure, even scientifically, where thoughts come from. We can't exactly say why some people think one way while others think another. These are the mysterious intangibles in our world that make life intriguing and challenge us to embrace their power and use them for good.

A non-prejudiced view of a client, which takes into account all of the aspects of the person, is an important key to helping her. By looking at her belief systems, lifestyle, history, genetics, and spiritual paradigm, a clearer context for treatment emerges. From that context, decisions can be made. Once I know all these dynamics of the person's reality, a pathway to health can be constructed. If the client understands the reasons and rationales, and experiences the benefits, she will be more able and be more inclined to follow that path to a healthy conclusion.

If we only take into account what can be proven, we miss the most beautiful things that make us human. Intuition is another example. As I've worked closely with more and more people in my practice, I've become aware of another part of myself: this intuitive sense that *knew* what needed to be said or done. At first I certainly did not trust this phenomenon. Gradually as I took more risks and started to trust the results I would see from them I was able to better hone and use this intuitive ability to help people. Sara is one such case.

Sara

This woman came to my clinic because she was angry all of the time. As we talked, she listed all of the "complaints" she had with her life. I listened patiently, as it is important, especially in the therapeutic environment, for a client to have her story "heard." After I had listened, none of the problems in this woman's life seemed to justify her miserable existence. Suddenly a thought struck me, and I abruptly asked her what her secrets were. She looked flabbergasted and somewhat angry. After eyeing me for a long time, she admitted that she had been having a series of affairs that her husband did not know about. She felt guilty and ashamed, but at the same time enjoyed the intensity she felt while with her current boyfriend. The conflict was making her sick.

I took a risk I was not comfortable with, but followed my intuition, making some suggestions I hoped would help her. I advised her to be honest with the people in her life and suggested that keeping secrets eventually makes one sick, physically and mentally, by adding undue stress in an already stressful life.

She was not happy when she left the office, and I was concerned I had taken the wrong approach. I had to remind myself that there was something bigger than both of us working here, and that if I was going to continue in the field, I was going to need to start trusting this intuitive process.

About a year later I was giving a talk at a local bookstore. After it was over a woman approached me and asked to talk. I sensed something familiar about her but could not remember any more than that. She reminded me who she was—it was Sara. She looked much different; her whole constitution had changed.

Sara told me that when she left my office she was mad and insulted. After she got home, she started thinking that maybe what I had told her had merit. She eventually confessed to her husband about the series of infidelities, figuring that even if he left her, the aggravating guilt she felt might be alleviated.

To her surprise, her husband forgave her. They recommitted to their marriage, began attending church and doing yoga together. She was eventually very happy with my willingness to be forthright with her. The process of healing for Sara started when I took a risk and followed my intuition, and, more importantly, she took the risk to become willing to take action.

This is an example of real holistic therapy. This situation did not need years of counseling or bottles of supplements. It required encouraging the client to take the right action according to *her* paradigm of right and wrong.

As you can surmise from this scenario, it was not comfortable for me to follow the inner prompting of my intuition. Even though I was scared, I did it. The result was beneficial not only to the client, but to other people with whom he had relationships as well.

Each one of us has this intuitive ability. We use it all of the time, often in unconscious ways. To make the effort to bring this ability to a conscious level and use it on a daily basis is often difficult, but it is well worth the courage and effort it takes.

As I started to use this intuiting in the clinic, I began to observe and experience regular predictable success helping people. I also learned a valuable lesson. Not everyone is ready, willing, or able to start working on herself when she first shows up.

Mary

Mary had come to my office at the suggestion of one of her friends. She was overweight and depressed. Her skin was a strange color and she felt miserable. The food she ate was, self-admittedly, of poor quality, and in general she looked sick. She had been to several doctors and none of them had found anything to explain her problems.

Mary had an unhealthy life style: she worked too many hours, had no close friends, and her home life was barren of affection. We discussed some healthier options. One simple suggestion was to drink more water. As I mentioned the idea, she made a contorted facial expression and turned away from me. Her body language told me she had stopped listening. When I confronted her she agreed that she had indeed tuned out, but now assured me she was willing to start making healthier choices in her life. I was not sure she really meant what she said. I have come to recognize when someone is not genuinely willing to make even the most basic healthy choices. They, for whatever reasons, are not ready to invest the time, effort, or money into achieving an optimally healthy lifestyle. Individuals must choose and commit to *the pursuit of health.*

Mary missed or cancelled her next two appointments. After that I did not see her again for 6 months. When she returned she had just been diagnosed with colon cancer. This impetus brought new willingness to support her medical treatment with a healthy lifestyle. She made a promise to take better care of herself, but sadly she was not able to follow through.

The friend who had referred her told me that Mary died 9 months later, still talking about the healthy changes she was going to make.

I took away from this painful example that there was nothing I could have done to help this woman at that time. Perhaps if she had been more willing, or had had more support or resources, the outcome may have been different. *Ultimately all healing comes from within, and each person is responsible for accepting and applying the help and information she receives.*

Another common example of staying stuck is the person who has some possible financial or emotional gain by staying sick or injured. The following are two short illustrations.

Accidents

On several occasions I have had to turn clients away because they would not let themselves get better. Their desire for financial gain was too strong. Vehicle accidents are a great example. When someone is involved in an accident and a lawsuit is involved, there can often be a conscious or unconscious choice not to get better, because the victim believs that if she gets better she will not get as much money. As a result, what may have been a few weeks or months of treatment stretches out, sometimes for years.

I have seen a few cases where this pattern was so severe that a form of mental illness manifested because of the conflict within the person. The desire to get far more money from the case than was actually reasonable keeps the victim in an injured state.

Sexual Harassment

It is possible in situations where strong emotion is involved, and a legal situation of some type is created, that physical results get exaggerated, and the ability of the body to heal is consciously or unconsciously hindered.

Kelly

Kelly worked in a law firm and was attracted to her male boss. She was flirtatious and seductive when in his presence. At a company party, when both were under the influence of alcohol, they kissed.

Some months later when the company was downsizing, Kelly was let go. The financial fear as a result of the termination was so distressing to her that she filed a lawsuit for sexual harassment against her prior boss and company for the incident at the office party. She cited emotional distress and depression as the result.

When I saw Kelly it was obvious that she was not doing well emotionally. She shared that she had put on unwanted weight and was not sleeping. It only took two visits before she *suggested that the cause might stem from the lawsuit she initiated. We uncovered that she did not truly feel justified in the charges against her prior employer and was manifesting symptoms to justify the charges and the financial compensation she desired.*

When it became clear to her what she was subconsciously doing, she dropped the lawsuits. Within a few weeks she lost the weight she had gained. Her "depression" cleared up, and she started a new job! I believe, had she won the lawsuit and received the money for which she had been asking, her physical and emotional condition may well have become permanent as a way of assuaging her guilt for the wrongful accusations.

My own evolution to optimal health later became the template for what I have designed in order to conduct my life's work: to help others. I call this design the Chadwell Method™. The 3 key components in this system are B-N-L:

- **Balance—A balanced physical structure within the body**
- **Nourishment—Ideal nutrition derived from food and supplements**
- **Love—Loving, yet honest, emotional support**

When I was first learning anatomy and studying the practice of bodywork, I was the recipient of hundreds of treatments. I needed most every one of them. Some were for my own physical body. I was full of physical pain from several vehicle accidents and full of toxicity from an unbalanced life style. Some of these treatments were not for me, but they allowed me to experience modalities that would be of benefit to others and to experience how the client would feel.

When I was first studying nutrition I applied the principles I learned to myself. Over time I completely changed my diet and way of eating. I started taking supplements which supported my constitutional type, and the results were so worthwhile that I still take several nutritional products every day, even though I eat a very healthy diet.

When I started to apply intuitional promptings to my own life, I was amazed at what happened. I never realized how much junk I was carrying around inside of me. By following subtle internal suggestions I was allowing to surface within me, often barely more than a whisper, I discovered quite a bit that was silently gnawing away at me. Frustration, past hurts, resentments, feelings of loss, and a number of other unnamed fears surfaced, so they could be eliminated. The next question was, "how?"

For some problems I felt I should seek out other professionals. For other issues I needed to write about them. Some required prayer. Others needed simply to be fully felt without seeking some form of outside relief.

Over time I felt clearer and more physically and emotionally stable. Ultimately my intuitive ability grew to become a very practical tool, one that I not only used in pursuit of my own journey to health, but that could be used with every client I saw. Equally important, as I worked with clients I found that as their bodies became healthier, and the emotional pressure they carried was being released, their own intuitive connections also started to develop. This continued to the point whereby they began to know what to do to reach optimal health without anyone's assistance.

A lot of time has passed since I started this process. I am very aware that I have been the major beneficiary of all the work. Life has a "trend line"—one of either improving or diminishing. For myself, as soon as I made a start *somewhere* in my life, the benefits were felt in other areas. When I eat better, my thoughts calm down. When I do yoga, I sleep better. When I began to forgive people and situations in the past, I was able to be more tolerant and forgiving of people around me in my present. This trend is self-perpetuating, but we all must make a start, and then assert consistency and follow-through. More times than not, having someone to guide this process is extremely valuable.

To be clear, for the people who come to me, I only help *them* to start the process. The natural healing ability that lies within every body is ready to spring up and do the work after some willingness and positive effort is demonstrated. Seeing this life force at work in my clients is one of my great joys, and indeed the most satisfying gift from my chosen life work.

You may ask, what does all this have to do with a book on relationships? Without a healthy body, a calm and clear mind, and the development of intuition, it is extremely difficult to exercise the consistent effort required for enjoyable and fulfilling relationships, be they with family, friends, lovers, or colleagues and workmates.

The time spent on self-improvement is deeply rewarding. Developing the above characteristic, especially intuition, helps to make all of life's problems more manageable. The peace of mind and confidence that you will become aware of is just the start of an adventure that continues to develop during your lifetime.

The Chadwell Method

The Chadwell Method is an exceptionally efficient system to evaluate a person's difficulties and then create a therapeutic plan that accurately addresses the areas of concern in order of priority. It acknowledges the equal importance of all aspects of the body, mind, emotion, spirit, and energetic field. The Chadwell Method lovingly supports the individual's change and at the same time allows client individuality to lead the therapeutic process.

Key Ideas to Remember

- There are many treatment styles or modalities. Find the one or combination that works for you.
- It must include structure, nutrition, and emotional support, as with the Chadwell Method™.
- B—N—L: Balance. Nourishment. Love.
- Find a practitioner you trust and with whom you feel comfortable, safe, and supported.
- Be willing to commit to your process for 6 to 12 months (and then, of course, apply consistency and follow-through).
- Realize that relationships are difficult (even in the best of circumstances), and a healthy body makes the process of growing and nurturing them easier.

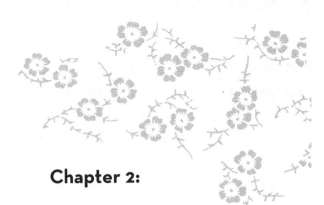

Chapter 2:

Be the Partner You Want to Have

**"Look at your own surroundings, good or bad,
for that is what influences you."
—Anthony Chadwell**

The Issues

The majority of people who come to me seem to feel a sense of loneliness and fear at a very deep level. We all have a tendency to minimize these feelings by seeking comfort outside of ourselves.

We humans attempt to avoid these feelings in myriad ways. We can alter the way we feel with any number of solutions. Researching and shopping online, or walking through a shopping center for hours becomes a form of "retail therapy."

Compulsive exercise in order to get an "endorphin high," is another example. Video games, gambling, watching pornography—these are all activities that alter our brains to produce chemicals that then make us feel better. Any activity that makes us feel good is likely to be repeated.

Relationships are a major area of our lives that can be manipulated to produce a change in how we feel. By focusing on what other people do, and how *they* behave, we can "get outside" of ourselves in a way. Doing this allows us to change the way we feel by distancing ourselves from our own internal awareness, an awareness that is often painful.

Most people I see are having difficulties in their relationships. The details can vary greatly. Below is a story that illustrates many typical concerns. More importantly, we can use this example to teach ourselves how to overcome some common obstacles.

Sydney

Sydney is successful in most outward areas of her life. She is attractive, earns good money, owns her own home, and has saved for retirement. She keeps herself looking good by exercising and dressing nicely.

Sydney's problem is that her thoughts are continually and obsessively focused on some man. When she is not in a relationship, she spends all of her time preparing to meet "Mr. Right" by changing her hairstyle, buying new clothes, and researching fabulous vacation spots.

When she is in a relationship, which is often just a short series of dates, she is happy, motivated, and busy planning future activities with her temporary new best friend.

Within a few weeks of their meeting, a pattern emerges: satisfaction in the relationship begins to diminish. Sydney becomes frustrated with the way he dresses or the amount of time he spends at work. This frustration builds, until they have an argument. The arguing alerts her into an awareness that the man she has chosen to be with may not be who or what she wants him to be.

As the relationship becomes stormier, Sydney obsesses about the characteristics or behaviors that do not fit her idealized vision of her perfect man, and she covertly, perhaps even subconsciously, sets about to change him into the type of man she wants.

As the man becomes aware of this manipulation, he feels pressure caused by Sydney's changing actions and flighty personality traits. As Sydney has experienced before, Mr. Right then uses whatever "tricks" have worked from his own past relationships to find a way out of this one.

Sydney becomes depressed and mopes through her days, alternatingly feeling sorry for herself, being angry with the guy, or wondering what she did wrong to "drive away such a good person."

In her case the man's departure usually takes the form of some type of betrayal. He does or does not do something he promised or she expected. She then claims that he misrepresented himself or deceived her in some way.

What really happened was that her desire to be in a relationship clouded her judgment. Sydney did not take the time to thoroughly get to know this person before determining if he really possessed all (or at least many) of the qualities she would seek. Her childlike desire for love and attention allowed her to overlook obvious signs of trouble. Serious warning signs, like drinking alcohol in the morning, bill collectors calling, and hostile relationships with his family members were easily explained away or ignored.

This typical cycle that Sydney finds herself in takes 3 weeks to 12 months to "complete." Sydney is always left feeling empty and depressed. After a period of time, she remembers the good feelings she had at the beginning of these relationships and becomes determined to have those feelings again. She tells herself, "this time will be different," and the cycle starts again.

In reality both Sydney and her partners are acting out unconscious patterns. She is taking actions which keep her from getting what she actually wants in a relationship and partner, but on the surface feels she is simply reacting to his "bad behavior."

The cycle works like this in her case: Sydney gets overly intimate very quickly after meeting someone, creating a type of enmeshment where she is losing herself in the good feeling she has and creates fanciful hopes about what the future might hold. She hopes to maintain this overly entangled state by using sex as glue to keep the man attached to her.

When problems arise, as they always do, Sydney overreacts, largely due to her long history of relationship trauma that has never really been addressed below the surface. Her overreaction is a "red flag" and frightening to the partner. He starts to recognize he is dealing with an "unstable person" and tries to find a way out. His pulling away creates more fear and frustration in her. She thus goes back and forth between being angry and then being overly nice so he won't leave the relationship. This behavior makes for even more craziness. Eventually some crisis catalyzes a breakup. Then the smoldering period starts.

During this time Sydney continues to be depressed and "done with men" entirely. She resolves not to date or involve herself in online dating. She begins to simply focus on "taking care of herself," but it is only a matter of time until the entire scenario is repeated.

This story illustrates how we create our realities by our own unconscious choices. If a relationship pattern happens more than twice, it is important to look to ourselves for the cause. We need to immediately set to work changing our own selves for the better if we want to have any chance of a meaningful and lasting relationship with someone who can support who we really are.

Sydney wants a reliable, considerate man, but she looks for him in bars and nightclubs late at night. She wants a man who is faithful to her, but she usually has sex with him on the first date. She wants an honest man, yet she begins to manipulate him from the very start.

These interactions are very complex and painful for the people involved. The pattern is complicated further if it involves the use of drugs or alcohol.

Another way to understand the idea we are talking about is to realize that we are attracted to other people who are roughly "equivalent in consciousness" to us. I like to think of this as two thermometers, side by side. The rise and fall of the mercury inside the thermometers represents the emotional maturity of two people. In order for the two people to be in a relationship, they must be within 10 degrees of each other. An "80" is never attracted to a "20." They are too far out of range; they do not relate. A "20" can relate with a "20," or a "50" with a "60," but in no way can an "80" relate with any long-term success to a "20." Because of their varying states of consciousness, they actually live in different emotional worlds and experience life quite differently. If the patterns are so different between a pair of people, the relationship may at first feel exciting, new, and adventurous, but later on it tends to become draining. Remember, we are talking about consciousness, our state of being, not our physical or environmental status.

When I talk about consciousness I am talking about the essential level of awareness the individual possesses—his ability to intuitively see the results of his actions and ability to evaluate the true essence of people and situations.

The idea behind this illustration is that if you want to attract a person of a higher caliber, the only way to do it *with lasting success* is to increase your own consciousness. This can be accomplished by consistently following the suggestions and guidelines throughout this book.

Many people trick themselves into thinking this idea does not apply. Often, this happens when the relationship offers some kind of "trade." An example might be when a younger, sexy woman gets into a relationship with a much older, wealthy man. This outside "trade" is physical attraction in exchange for financial security. Sometimes this works, because the "trade" is more important to the individuals than is the intimacy that might be found with someone in a closer resonance than theirs.

Another example is when two wealthy people or two people in the same career get together. The "trade" in this case is mutual support for something they both value, i.e. money or career success.

The Root Cause

The causes of this pattern are uncomfortable feelings, fear (of being alone, for instance), and the hope that association with another person (any person) can eliminate the discomfort and fear. This cycle is perpetuated by repeatedly becoming involved with a person who does not, at his essential self, have the ability or desire to give us what we think we need.

We usually learn this escape mechanism from people around us or from within our families. If we had a good childhood, we expect to recreate that in our adult life, though not everyone who came from a happy home has the ability to reproduce that experience with another person. Even fairly functional homes generally have some areas of psychological deficiency. These short falls (or lack of discerning principles) can set an adult up for problems when trying to replicate his childhood home environment.

If our childhood was unhealthy in some way, we may set out to create our "idealized" future without having the necessary skills to do so. This pattern is more common and also more problematic. We don't know what we don't know. We cannot easily recreate something we never had to begin with. This is often why we keep reenacting damaging patterns with other people.

In either example, the desire to build a comfortable environment is, understandably, a powerful driving force.

The idea that we attract what we feel we need, and thus continue unhealthy patterns, is not an easy idea to accept when it involves you. People fit together like two cogs on a pair of gears. Each provides the missing "metal" the other one needs to function.

A common example is the alcoholic who needs to have an enabler to allow him to continue to drink. It can be a wife, a parent, or an organization, but an alcoholic *needs* that other person for the game to continue. Someone has to call work and tell the boss he is sick when he is really hung over. Someone is required to work and pay the bills when the alcoholic is not able.

In the type of relationship we are talking about in Sydney's case, the woman who stays stuck and frustrated in this pattern actually subconsciously creates it. She *needs* a man who is not emotionally available, otherwise this cycle (which I have coined a drama-loop™) cannot continue. She *needs* a man who reacts to her erratic behavior by pulling away so she can feel the strong emotion of abandonment and "trade on" a sense of victimization. If these affection/aggression cycles did not ignite, the pattern of "being stuck" could not continue. Other dynamics can certainly come into play, but the general requirement is that two people must react to each other in a predictable and unconscious way so that the alternating cycle of good feelings, leading to frustration, leading to loss, leading to looking for more good feeling, can continue.

The Solution

It is important to keep in mind the cause of these unconscious behaviors. We are often only aware of the *problems* these relationships create—again, these are the symptoms, not the root cause. We generally don't see our part in it. The conflicts and misfortunes are things "done to us." Reading a book like this one helps us see the larger picture of our own roles in the scenarios. The courage it takes to do the work within oneself is often more of a fear than just continuing, in this case, in the abandonment cycle.

Having someone point out these patterns in a loving and supportive way, as they are taking place, can be very useful. This only works if we are open and willing to take guidance regarding our behavior. This period of awareness may be uncomfortable. It brings up the very feelings we have been so busy trying to avoid.

Here's how to start:

- **Make a written list of characteristics you value** and that you seek in other people with whom you wish to surround yourself.
- **After writing this list, you must take an honest look at yourself** and see where you fall short of these in your own life. This will take meditative and quiet reflection time with yourself.
- **More urgently, you need to *develop* these characteristics in yourself and demonstrate them *through your own actions* in your life.** If you are clingy, you need to find ways to develop a healthy independence. If consistency is what you want in other people, you must practice ways of being more consistent yourself. Whatever is on the list that *you* think is

important, must be developed in *yourself* first. Then you will know if these persons you meet really have this quality, or if they are attempting to appear more than they genuinely are.

Relationships with other people should be an important *part* of our lives, not our "entire life." To be well-rounded human beings, we must develop strong "inner worlds" in addition to our "outer worlds."

If we spend too much time and effort focusing on any one relationship, it is a good sign that our life is out of balance.

It is important for healthy human beings to do some kind of productive activity every day. We all need time for hobbies or outside interests. We all need to take care of our physical bodies and have a healthy network of friends.

By developing a well-rounded life with many important parts that make up the whole, we do not become overly reliant on any one person or part for our happiness or self-worth.

I wrote about the importance of intuition in Chapter 1. This cannot be emphasized enough: going through the process of clearing the body of emotional and physical toxins is crucial to developing this important intangible ability called intuition.

Once this intuitive ability is brought to consciousness, we have a real tool to help us develop our relationships in healthy, balanced ways, as well as to "fix" our relationship problems. We do this by being able to "see down the road." In other words, we start making decisions based on something other than our immediate wants and needs. This is conventionally known as "emotional maturity" or emotional wisdom.

If you want something you must give it away. This important spiritual axiom applies to relationships as well as to other areas of our lives. If you want to be loved, practice being *sincerely* loving to everyone you meet! If you want people to be patient and forgiving, you are required to behave that way with the people in your life. More difficult yet, if you want people to trust you, start developing trust in others. Not a foolish trust that could get you into trouble, but a bigger, more encompassing trust in the general goodness of mankind and of the beauty of life in general.

Ultimately, we must learn that security and happiness does not come from other people. It comes only from a wisely developed maturity that each and every one of us is capable of.

One more point: this chapter, for the most part, has been talking about primary, romantic relationships. I want to remind you that these same principles can (and should) be applied to all of our relationships—at work, school, with our own children, siblings, and even parents.

Key Ideas to Remember

- The cause of relationship difficulties is often subconscious; we tend to be only aware of the pain.
- Create a written list of the characteristics you want in others.
- Develop these qualities in *yourself*.
- Relationships should only be *part* of a balanced life.
- Permanent peace and lasting security does not come from another person.

Chapter 3:

Recreating the Familiar—
Even When It Hurts

"No one can push your buttons better than
the people who install them."
-Anonymous

The Issues

How many times have you talked with a friend as he told you a story like this:

He thought, at the beginning of his current relationship, that he had chosen a good partner. This partner was nothing like the last person he was with. Yet, after some time he realizes his current partner IS exactly like the last partner he'd had. (Different "packaging" but with the same recurring issues.) In fact, as he looks back these issues were just like the ones that arose with the last several partners he'd chosen.

Perhaps this example applies to you. If so, you're not alone. Many people subconsciously continue to engage in non-supportive relationships over and over again and do not know why.

When a person knows she is repeating an unhealthy pattern, she may try to improve her choices by picking someone who, from the outside at least, looks and seems extremely different from the person with whom she just broke up. The new person may come from a different socio-economic background; he may even have more or less education than the prior love interest. These differences trick us into thinking that we have made a real change for the better.

What we may not know is that the part of us doing the choosing is broken. Apparent free will in the matter has actually been eclipsed by prior experiences. Try as we might, we end up with the same outcome in all of our relationships. I have a solution to breaking this pattern, but first some more case studies:

Jerome

Jerome is a good-looking guy in his late forties. He has been involved in numerous relationships over the last 10 years, since his divorce from his first wife. The "exterior" of all of his new partners over this last decade appear very different. Some were educated; some were not. One was very successful in business; others were stay-at-home moms. Several were much younger than he, while others were around his own age. The physical appearances of these women varied greatly, as did the circumstances in which these women lived. One thing was very *consistent, though: they all eventually behaved the same way.*

After Jerome became involved with these women, within a few weeks they would exhibit extreme mood fluctuations. These mood swings coincided with their menstrual cycles. It seemed their moods would shift dramatically. As the relationships progressed these swings would show up for one or two weeks out of each month. The changes in mood were usually some form of anger. The women would be argumentative, then begin yelling, having tantrums, storm out of the house, etc. Jerome would "check" his own behavior to analyze what dynamic he might have brought to the table: was it something he'd caused? Why so much erratic and seemingly irrational behavior?

Some of these women showed this extreme emotional trouble in the form of depression. They would become sullen and withdrawn. Without exception, none of these women were willing to seek any treatment or counsel for their conditions. They were unwilling to see or explore that perhaps a likely cause of their "crazy" behavior was due to hormonal imbalance.

The turmoil these relationships caused in Jerome's emotional life over the years was very draining. He did not sleep well, and he often turned to alcohol and overworking as ways to escape his uncomfortable feelings and circumstances.

Jerome would engage in what would become a familiar cycle of repeatedly breaking up then getting back together again. After many rounds of this on-gain-off-again behavior, some event would eventually precipitate a final breakup.

Jerome would show up at my clinic expressing anger not only toward his current partner but also toward himself. He would express confusion but also feel victimized. Each new relationship would eventually end in disappointment and place him back in this now recurring role of victim, whereby he "couldn't understand what went wrong."

My counsel was to suggest that he not date for six months to a year; take a break. During this time he should do the deep introspective work required to once and for all, root out "the why" behind his continuing failed romantic relationships. I suggested he try to analyze personality traits of the women he chose, to understand if there might be some common patterns causing the ultimate recurring incompatibility.

Jerome would agree this was a good idea. He would remind himself that since his divorce he had never really spent any time by himself for reflection or future planning. He would agree it was time to give himself some "down time" for solitude and keener self-knowledge; this time would be different.

Within a week he would again be dating someone he had recently met and been attracted to. The intensity of that first blush of new relationships and dating shut out authentic opportunities for him to look below the surface of his life and determine what the real problem was.

Jerome was unaware that at a very deep and unconscious level he was repeatedly choosing women who were emotionally unstable due to imbalances in their hormones.

Eventually Jerome did commit to a written assignment designed to help him determine when he first remembered having this type of inconsistent relationship with a woman. He unearthed a similar pattern he experienced with his mother during his formative years as a child, remembering the frustration he felt toward her erratic behavior. Some days she would be extremely happy; other days she would stay in her bedroom all day. Periods of excessive discipline, including harsh physical punishment, would be followed by episodes of no parental supervision at all.

Jerome had fallen into the trap of recreating a previous childhood environment in his adult life, something that was familiar though not necessarily satisfying or healthy.

Diane

Diane first came into my office because of how she was reacting to situational stress in her life. After talking for a few minutes it became apparent that the majority of the stress she felt derived from her financial situation. This anxiety was beginning to take its toll on her overall physical health and well being.

She explained that during her prior relationship, with a mechanic who "spent every penny he made," they were always broke. While he had good earning potential, as a couple they just couldn't seem to make ends meet. When this relationship came to an end Diane made a conscious decision to date a man who made "a lot of money." She accomplished this in short order and in fact became involved with a business executive who made over two hundred thousand dollars per year. Diane assumed that with this salary, along with what she earned, they would be very comfortable financially. What she did not know was that this new man, with whom she was now living, was a poor money manager. While he made a good income, he had no idea how to manage his finances. He would invest in some "sure deal" or some venture with a friend and would repeatedly lose money.

These losses, along with a luxurious life style of expensive meals and travel, put them in a continual state of financial crisis.

Diane illustrates a very common delusion, that if you change the partner you are with, you will change the circumstances around you.

Financial environment is one of those areas in our lives that we tend to recreate over and over. Often, if we grew up in a household that was always in financial chaos, like Diane, we unconsciously find people and situations that help us live in that same emotional environment.

Not everyone grew up in a home that had financial lack. A segment of the population has never experienced the fear of financial insecurity. These people live in a reality that provides plenty of money. As these children grow, they consciously or subconsciously choose mates who help support this financial reality. One of the problems that arises with this group is that they often "sell out" other important parts of their emotional lives in order to maintain that financial security to which they've become accustomed. It is possible for these people to have loveless relationships or to be in relationships with mates to whom they are not physically or sexually attracted.

Another scenario that produces distressing adult relationships is when one has been exposed to incest or some other form of sexual abuse as a young person. This type of abuse actually changes the energetic construct of the victim's physical and emotional body, presenting many mind/body challenges in adulthood.

Many women and men who have experienced traumatic events such as these have a tendency to subconsciously avoid intimate relationships, preferring to protect themselves from scenarios and situations that might yield a recurrence of the pain. This doesn't mean they don't engage in relationships, but rather that they may be in relationships devoid of true intimacy. Others often unwittingly recreate environments that allow for repeated abuse.

Jill

A youth counselor molested Jill at her church when she was 14. She held anger and resentment from this traumatic event and the poor way it was handled by the church after it was exposed. A lawsuit ensued that provided Jill with some funds for therapy in her teens.

I met Jill in her late thirties. By this time she had experienced several more instances of sexual abuse from strangers and boyfriends. She came to me distraught and feeling hopeless about all men.

Jill had no idea that the initial abuse had actually changed her "essence." In a way it was like putting out a flag attracting other men who were also capable of abusing her.

As Jill and I worked together, she not only needed to acknowledge the obvious recurring pattern, but also had to look at the predominant "thought field environment" she was creating that perpetuated her victimization.

People who are raised in an environment where the major caregivers are emotionally absent also recreate this environment later in life. The emotional absence can be from substance abuse or other trauma that the caregivers have experienced themselves. They are, consequently, emotionally unavailable for the children.

Kids who are raised in this type of environment gravitate toward emotionally unavailable adult partners. It seems the lack of constant emotional support with which they are familiar is more (subconsciously) comfortable than the effort it takes to bring this repeating pattern to a conscious level, and to then develop the skills necessary to change their lives for the better.

Another scenario I have observed, from which can spring disconnected adult relationships, is from people who have been raised in families with either a strong military or corporate connection. For example, having a parent who responds to strict authoritarian regulation in the military, and who then transfers that philosophy to educating his children, can create a similar distancing of emotional support for the child.

One more major area of patterning is infidelity in a relationship. If we were exposed to infidelity during our development we may recreate that experience in future relationships. If a parent or someone important to us cheated on a partner and violated his trust, it is possible that at some level we may feel authorized to do the same thing.

The opposite can also be true. If we were close to someone who was a victim of betrayal, we may develop a subconscious affinity to that painful situation, from a twisted and latent sense of loyalty or sympathy. This connection may ironically put us in a position to later be betrayed by someone else.

So far we have been discussing fairly severe examples. But it is important to note that the environment from which we learn does not need to have been that extreme to have negative effects. Having come up in an environment that was filled with anxiety or fear (for whatever cause) is enough to distort our sense of reality and/or our sense of what is possible.

Some families are overly focused on emotional ties to food, often equating food with love, comfort, and attention. Later in life when we feel uncomfortable, we may find people who or environments that, literally, feed us. Not only can this keep us from facing important real feelings that comprise the full life experience, it can lead to many different eating disorders.

Emotional triangles are another area of concern. If a family has a "favorite" member and other members are aware of it, it can set up a pattern of tolerating unfair or unequal relationships at home or work. This inequality is a form of abuse. The setting becomes familiar and others will often take advantage of it.

If the developmental environment involves any type of secrecy, it is possible to pass that dysfunction on to other people without their knowing it.

Sylvia

Sylvia came to my Health Center because of digestive issues. She had grown up with a feeling of what she described as a constant underlying "dread" or impending doom. She had always known that her family had serious secrets. Often, when she walked into a room the other people there would abruptly stop talking. When she was little she was aware that people would speak in a kind of code when she or her siblings were around.

She felt all of this tension in her body but could not pinpoint its cause. Over time she developed a "stomach ache" and was taken to the doctor several times. The doctor was never able to find anything wrong with her; she was eventually told it was "all in her head."

By the time I saw her she had discovered that her grandfather had committed suicide, and her family was very ashamed of this fact. The incident was kept under wraps, never spoken about to the children, because her well-meaning family did not want to upset them.

This may have been appropriate up to a certain age, but the fact that this secrecy continued until her mid-twenties proved to be very dysfunctional for Sylvia.

Sylvia felt betrayed by her family's secrecy and was angry as an adult because no one had connected the stress in her formative years with her ongoing digestive issues.

I have found in my years of practice that most digestive issues have an emotional origin. By bringing her family's secrets out into the open, Sylvia was able to look at them objectively. I was able to help her by utilizing techniques which calm the sympathetic nervous system, the part of our nervous system that regulates digestion when the body is stressed.

I also came up with a nutritional protocol that helped rebuild the damage that was present in her digestive tract from years of stress.

The Solution

It is a simple truth that we are all products of our environment to some extent. It is also true that no human life is without some problems or emotional pain. We can understand that we all have lessons to learn when it comes to dealing with other people and building/maintaining relationships. The examples I have shared are not designed to cast blame or point fingers away from oneself for any afflictions or consequences one is suffering, but are meant to help shed light on possible *root causes* for one's dissatisfaction, unhappiness, or "dis-ease" with the circumstances in one's life.

Here's where your work begins. The intent of this section is that we become able to determine our own subconscious involvement in the problems that seem to reoccur over and over again in our lives, to bring this to a conscious level, so we can then determine our own corrective behavior to improve our lives.

First, we need to reduce the intensity of the situation. This is the only way to find the space to do the deep introspective work that is needed to unlock the secrets of the past. Find a nurturing environment that helps lower the sympathetic tone of your nervous system.

This is an environment that feels safe and has little or no stress. It may be a retreat setting, a park or other outdoor area, or a quiet place in your own home. The important part is to feel secure and not threatened by your surroundings. The sympathetic nervous system is the part of your nervous system that prepares you for fight or flight. It raises your heart rate and sends blood to your muscles. You can tell your sympathetic nervous system is relaxing when your heart rate decreases and you feel a general sense of relaxation. The most efficient way to do this is by focusing on your breathing slowing your breath.

Identify what emotional state you experience most of the time. Do you feel panicky? Do you feel scared, depressed, or anxious—or a combination of all of these emotions? This is important; take your time. Really let yourself feel that predominant feeling that currently "guides your day-to-day." It won't kill you to feel it, even though your head may tell you otherwise! This will require real "quiet time" with yourself, so you must be ready to invest in this "gift"—to allow for introspection unhindered by day-to-day distractions.

Next, identify at what point in your life you first remember experiencing this predominant, driving feeling. This usually goes back to a period in your life in which you felt confused or overwhelmed. Any period of overwhelm creates a stress reaction in the body. This stress reaction is a protective mechanism that changes our brain chemistry to give us the highest chance of survival. It may dull a situation to protect us from feeling everything "too much all at once," (like when someone faints). Often our subconscious inclination is to simply "shut down" our authentic emotional selves, whereby we "react" passively in lieu of "proactively" addressing how we want our healthy life experiences to go.

The stress reaction may also, conversely, heighten our awareness levels so that we see and experience everything hyper-acutely. Either way, we are temporarily not ourselves. These altered physiological and emotional states make us vulnerable to misinterpretation of an event and allow this altered view of life to permanently change our existence. Here's where we get "stuck." It is this altered life view that forces us to unconsciously recreate those intense emotional environments in later relationships, ironically processing these events as "normal" or comfortable, and not consciously understanding that we are participants in our own cycles of unsatisfying outcomes.

I sometimes use the example of living in different socioeconomic realities to explain the way people's views can be different. Someone who has always lived in poverty often has a very difficult time relating to someone who lives a life of affluence. The opposite can also be true of someone who has always had more economic resources than they need: they might find it hard to intrinsically understand what it is like to live with financial lack. These are two different realities. The same is true of traumatic emotional overlays™. (This is a term I coined to explain a disruption of the normal functioning of the body at any level, due to a prior period of overwhelm.) These cause an altered awareness of life to the individual experiencing them.

From my own history I learned that it was normal to keep secrets from people close to you. I was raised in an environment with what I call emotional-triangles. These triangles of emotion are not equal between the people involved. In my case, I held a lot of my mother's secrets from my stepfather. I also continue to keep a few of his from my mother. This was very "normal" and an unspoken expectation in my household. Later in life it was very natural for me to keep secrets from other people close to me, even if the outcome was hurtful to all involved.

I also felt the need to anticipate what the people around me were feeling. This required me to become hyper-vigilant to my environment. I could easily determine someone's state of mind and his/her primary emotion. This capacity allowed me to feel safe, when I was young, as I could adjust my behaviors to achieve a desired outcome of a sense of comfort in my surroundings.

These abilities still exist *in a healthy way* in my professional life. I can easily keep the confidences of all of my clients, because I have learned the difference between keeping unhealthy secrets, which breed unhappiness, and beneficial confidences, which promote a safe healing environment. I am also able to "read" what people are feeling very quickly.

Knowing when a problem started is important, but one must do more. ***The next step is to learn to be present in your own life.*** This allows you to discover the emotional overlay as soon as it starts to happen. It is like when your mind starts to tell you a story. Every time the story is told you short cut it, or cut off a little bit of the ending. After some time the story gets condensed, shorter and shorter. Eventually you can tell when "a story" is going to start. At that very moment you think about something else, thus short-circuiting the story and its effects entirely. With the emotional overlay your job is to notice when those strong emotions begin to well up in you. The more you practice, the more you become aware. The more you become aware, the sooner you can "catch" the emotional overlay.

One way you can develop this ability is by doing what I call CPR. CPR is part of the Chadwell Method™ and is a fast, effective, and easy way to bring yourself into the present moment.

C=Calm

P=Present

R= Reverent

It is a training tool for the mind. Here is how it works.

Calm yourself by breathing slowly in through your nose. Pay attention to the way the air feels as it hits the back of the nasal passage. This is the area in the back of your mouth close to your throat. This action activates the parasympathetic nervous system.

This is the part of your nervous system that allows you to relax and digest your food. It provides a feeling of peace.

Being **Present** is attained by softening your visual gaze. You do this by slightly de-focusing your eyes. Do not look at anything in particular. Make your eye movements very slow. This calms the central nervous system.

Being **Reverent** is an attitude you experience when you've ascertained an appropriate perspective on your life. This state of reverence allows all things to be as they are *in this moment*. It is complete acceptance of the present. It allows you to be human; it allows others to be human as well. It allows us to be part of something bigger than ourselves. Something powerful takes over when we do CPR: we slow down, and this allows us to simply make better choices.

I manifest a state of reverence when I slow my breathe and take a moment to remember that I am an important part of an incredibly vast universe. Simply reminding myself how fortunate I am to be alive and aware of that fact helps me experience the grandeur of my own life experience. That quickly translates into reverence for me. You may find another way to bring about this state of reverence. It is important because being in this state gives us a different, more humble, perspective.

By being aware and taking the steps necessary to free yourself to simply be present, you will be amazed at how you are able to stop or short-circuit patterns that have left you feeling overwhelmed in the past. You will stop reacting unconsciously and will allow yourself to enjoy a better quality life and to pass on this education to other people around you.

Key Ideas to Remember:

- You cannot judge the reality of a person by his looks or circumstances.
- Make a written list of traumatic events that happened to you AND people close to you.
- Make note of your age when these events took place.
- Reflect on and search out what needs of yours were not met because of these events.
- Cross-reference your repeating relationship problems with those unfulfilled needs.
- Learn how to fulfill those needs now in healthy ways. Seek outside help, if necessary.
- Practice CPR: Calm-Present-Reverent

Chapter 4:

I Have Everything. Now What?

"Gratitude is the antidote for all uncomfortable thought."
-Anthony Chadwell

The Issues

This chapter focuses on the frustrated people who have pieced together an enjoyable exterior life but still feel the nagging discontent of an unfulfilling relationship. I mention this topic because it is important. People in this situation do not feel they have a right to talk about the frustration they experience because their lives "by comparison" seem so well balanced (from the outside looking in) to everyone who knows them. Our secrets keep us sick.

For these people material circumstances are often very good, so they feel they are being "complainers" or unrealistic in their expectations if they even mention the frustration they feel. This awkwardness and inner struggle can keep them isolated. Often they present themselves around friends and other people as having a picture-perfect life. Keeping up this pretense isolates their "inner person" even more.

Most of us have a drive to create an enjoyable environment, one that is fulfilling and provides the necessities of life. The "necessities" vary with each individual. Some only want enough to exist. Others expect a full and happy relationship experience and abundance in every area of their lives.

Occasionally it would seem that "some people get everything they want in life." But in reality most of us must be content with compromise: a degree of successes combined with some areas that need improvement. Real relationships are a form of continuous conscious compromise.

Liz

Liz met a nice man. He was an attorney and successful financially. She worked hard, and between them they enjoyed an affluent lifestyle. They eventually married and purchased a wonderful home in an exclusive neighborhood. When they initially met there was talk of "children in the future." Liz assumed the family she wanted would come in due course.

As years passed the topic of children was always dealt with as "a likelihood," but not something they should do now. She and her husband enjoyed travel and many other luxuries in their life together sans children, but Liz could not help feel something was wrong. She had an underlying depressed feeling that rarely left her. She started to gain weight.

As her husband became more and more successful in the legal field, he spent more time away from home; he was out of town many days each month. All of this alone-time gave Liz the opportunity to think. She realized she had developed a deep resentment of her husband and herself for not having children. When Liz pushed the issue with her husband, it became clear that he was more interested in his growing career than in becoming a father.

The reality of this forced Liz to make a difficult decision: either leave her husband and find a man who would start a family with her, or stay with her husband and enjoy the comfortable lifestyle with which she was familiar. Result: she bought a dog.

Not just any dog, but an imported $20,000 something-or-other breed that was all the rage. She was happy for a while because she had "something to love." It was not long before she needed to find a mate for the first dog she purchased. She then remodeled the house so she could have a dog nursery.

Dogs became her business. Liz bred and sold these animals all over the country and had some significant success with showing them. This obsession went on for years. Eventually everything in Liz's life revolved around her dogs.

When I met Liz she was 80 pounds overweight, depressed, and her husband was "never home." She told me her house smelled of dogs so bad she had no friends and was isolated, even from her family. The emotional emptiness and resentment she felt over not having children had morphed into a very dysfunctional situation.

I have seen similar emotional emptiness get channeled into other forms of addictive behavior: excessive exercise, over work, obsession with other hobbies or habits.

This emptiness, in spite of external success, can also occur in homes where children *are* present. It isn't "children" per se, or not having children, that is the fundamental issue. In fact, it is possible to often use children as a distraction from the basic emptiness in a primary relationship.

When children are the primary focus that excludes everything else, the family unit can become unbalanced. The parents get so overly enmeshed that the child is (or children are) all the parent or parents think or talk about.

The children are usually not lovingly disciplined and commonly "rule" the home with their emotional outbursts or unmanageable behavior. Regularly, an inordinate amount of the family income is spent on indulging the children in some way.

Sometimes these hidden areas appear early in a relationship. Other times these emotional vulnerabilities only appear after some time or under certain circumstances.

Scott's case provides another example of "having it all" yet still finding oneself frustrated and feeling empty.

Scott

Scott married a very cute young woman, and for 10 years they were very happy. As his wife turned 35 something happened with her self-image, and she became dissatisfied with her appearance. She was naturally attractive and accustomed to attention, so when her natural aging process began and her looks began to change, she was not prepared for her reactions. She started to work out more, then insisted on breast enhancement surgery. The surgery was successful, and for a while she again received the attention to which she was accustomed. After the novelty of the breast surgery wore off, she was once again frustrated with her looks.

She began to employ various injectable cosmetic enhancers to minimize the evidence of aging. Up to this point, Scott did not see a problem with his wife's behavior.

But once his wife began having a series of cosmetic facial surgeries that dramatically changed her appearance, Scott became naturally concerned. Her looks appeared "unreal" to him, and he found it troubling to even look at his wife. The sexual intimacy they had always shared started to wane. Scott became embarrassed to take his wife to social events because of their friends' reactions.

People stared at her in public. Her impression was that she looked good and that other women envied her. Scott, on the other hand, was aware that she looked unnatural, and even desperate, and the stares his wife was receiving were actually a form of ridicule. Sadly, though predictably, the distance between Scott and his wife deepened as his embarrassment of her superficial transformation grew.

It is not likely that Scott could have anticipated that this situation would develop in his marital partnership. He had no idea that his wife placed so much importance on her physical look, or that natural aging would stir up such vulnerability or lead to her extreme behavior.

Scott's story is an example of a life with "quality problems." He and his wife had more than enough money for the basics of food, clothing, and shelter, yet they fell prey to an unfortunate situation because of the hidden vulnerability in Scott's wife's self-esteem. Had there been an awareness of her emotional vulnerability earlier in the marriage, perhaps there could have been some intervention to help his wife understand how the aging process was affecting her subconscious state and to have found a way to build her self esteem in a healthy way.

The expression of imbalance in a relationship does not need to be so severe. Take this next study, for instance.

Carly

Carly is married to a busy executive. Her husband travels and often works late. Carly is an alcoholic who has been in recovery for the last 11 years. She realizes that her marriage is not emotionally supportive but has made a conscious decision that she will stay in the relationship because it meets all of her financial, and some of her emotional, needs.

Carly attends 12-step meetings and has many friends. She realizes that her history of substance abuse, coupled with prior infidelities, could jeopardize her marriage. She certainly does not want to relapse or become unfaithful with her present husband.

Carly knows she needs to keep herself busy with constructive activities, so she volunteers for many recovery-related positions in her area. This occupies about 20 hours per week. She also teaches exercise classes at the local gym. Also, in order to divert her attention away from her loneliness when she is home by herself, she often "surfs the internet" until 2 or 3 o'clock in the morning.

Initially, I saw Carly because of complaints related to insomnia. She has matured considerably from her drinking days, but she has not yet developed enough maturity and self-confidence to resolve the real underlying problems in her life.

Until she is able to talk honestly with her husband to see if they can come to some compromise for his over-working and her loneliness, she will continue to "over-distract" in some area of her life, in order to avoid the strong feelings of isolation she feels in her marriage.

These are just a few examples of people who, while they have apparent success in most areas of their lives, cover up or compromise, when it comes to their primary relationships.

The Root Cause

People usually get into these lopsided associations because they "sell-out" or betray themselves early in the relationship. Often, some important need was neglected or denied out of insecurity or self-interest. For instance, a common situation is one where financial security is perceived to be more important than the ability to easily communicate with your partner. Another common choice is to regard sexual attraction or the act of sex itself as so crucial that the emotional stability of a partner is not properly considered.

This is not the worst possible situation in which to find yourself. In the above examples it is important to remember that *most* of these persons' needs seem to be sufficiently met. The overall satisfaction in these people's lives is still rather high.

The relationships that come under this heading often need a refining and clarifying process. It certainly does not mandatorily mean putting an end to the relationship.

At other times, the primary frustration only becomes obvious after several years of being together. The awareness grows out of a maturity that was not present when they first met. There may be no way to know, for example, that a wife may become interested in teaching, or that a husband may find an interest in music. Initially this couple may have been involved in the basics of relationship building, often focusing on making money, creating a home, or raising children.

Priorities often shift with aging. The passing of time allows for a deeper reflection of what is important in life. The goals of a person in his fifties can be much different than someone in her thirties, and vice versa.

With age comes the tendency to be more internally oriented. The subtleties of feeling kindness, compassion, and peace of mind may become very important as someone ages. If this process of internalization develops at a different rate in a couple, a mismatching may develop. For example, if one partner is really interested in building a business and the other person wants to travel abroad, a conflict may arise.

Consciousness of the brevity of life forces a reprioritization. We become aware of the time we have wasted with useless pursuits and ego-driven desires. We may perceive this as a loss that leads to a sense of grief. This feeling of loss further complicates the relationship.

We vow that we will stop squandering time and only do what is really important. Problems arise when the definition of "important" is different between partners.

The Solution

Whenever the opportunity for a relationship presents itself, exhibit as much honesty as possible in that moment without being abusive to yourself or others. The seeds for future discontent are sown early in a relationship by withholding important information that should be shared or by denying significant aspects of ourselves in order to appear better or more important than we feel we really are.

If need be, get help in determining what is really important to you. Seek out a professional or someone you trust to help you identify characteristics in yourself that could later lead to trouble. Equally as important is to discover attributes that are mandatory in a mate; then be willing and discerning enough to leave a relationship in the early phases if it becomes obvious that those characteristics are not found in the potential partner. Be clear and honest with who you are and the areas in which you will not compromise. It is much easier emotionally, not to mention more efficient, to screen future partners by these important characteristics.

When you are not sure what these important points are, here are some guidelines to make them easier to determine.

1. **Ask yourself what frustrates you**. You can also ask someone you know to tell you what you complain about the most. These isues are obviously important to you.
2. **At the first sign of frustration or fear, stop and acknowledge that fact**. Take a moment and tune-in to these uncomfortable feelings.
3. **Analyze what is going on.** This can be done by journaling or by an end-of-day review. This review is best done at night

right before going to sleep when the details of the day are present and the environment in the home is quieter. Evaluate everything that disturbs you. Look for common themes. Have you acted in a selfish way? Did someone trigger a past hurt? Are you afraid of somebody or some circumstance? Identify the patterns that influence you and lead to uncomfortable emotions or in appropriate actions. Identifying these is an important first step in resolving them.

4. **Monitor your emotions for uncomfortable patterns**. If you feel insecure or angry most of the time, find out why! Professionals can be very useful in helping to crystalize, into a simple form, all of the crazy and conflicting thoughts that can run through your mind at any given moment.

5. **Maintain communication with your partner**. Don't pout or isolate. These forms of emotional manipulation don't work in the long run. They are insulting, and the other person will find a way to retaliate in the future. At any rate these immature strategies do not provide a consistent or trustworthy form of communication. Be the bigger person when the situation requires it. Humility is the path to happiness.

6. **Ask for what you need**. It is important to get your needs meet in a healthy way, hopefully from your partner. If that is not possible find a safe, appropriate, and healthy option. This may be from friends or a professional therapist.

7. **If at all possible find out what is important to your partner and give your partner what he needs**. The spiritual axiom "as you give, so shall you receive" is nowhere truer than in a close intimate relationship. Become consciously aware of your partner's needs. When it becomes obvious to one or both

of you that there is some aspect that cannot be realistically met, acknowledge that reality.

8. Seek some constructive and healthy way to fill that void.

There is no excuse to selfishly fulfill those unmet needs at the expense of others. That includes substance abuse, financial mismanagement, or infidelity in a relationship. If you are not willing to fulfill your needs by acting in a mature and healthy way that does not hurt other people, it may be wise to get out of the relationship. You owe it to all involved to do the right thing, even if temporarily someone must be hurt or you must experience a sense of loneliness from the break-up.

However, if you are aware of the vacuum in your life and you know you are going to stay in the relationship, wisely search out options that satisfy your needs in a productive way.

Many constructive choices are available for people who choose to stay in a relationship. I know several people who started learning how to play a musical instrument in order to constructively fill in times they were alone, or felt alone. There are many benefits of music. The focus required occupies their minds, and the association with other people interested in the same type of music allows for positive social contact.

Other choices include continuing one's education, supporting civic organizations, and working for one's church or some charitable organization.

If your tendency is to isolate, force yourself to become part of a group that allows this underdeveloped part of you to form and evolve. If you find it difficult to be by yourself and are always surrounded by people, seek some activity that teaches you to be more independent, like meditation or hiking.

The idea is to proactively seek a balanced life the best possible way you can, given your current circumstances.

Every relationship has relationship problems. That is the nature of two people being in association with each other. Big or small, these problems must be deliberately dealt with before those suppressed needs cause unnecessary pain and bigger problems for you and everyone else involved.

Key Ideas to Remember

- Hold your relationship with love and integrity to minimize pain and maximize the joy life has to offer.
- Be grateful for the many good aspects of your relationship; practice grace in and appreciation of these.
- Carefully evaluate areas in your life that are not fulfilled by a partner.
- If the relationship is going to continue, find a way to satisfy your unmet needs in healthy and honest ways.
- If it is impossible to live in the current relationship move on in a graceful and loving way

Chapter 5:

Addicted To the Drama—
The Cycle of Staying Stuck

"Until you can sit contentedly by yourself,
for a long time, you have no business imposing
your pathology on someone else."
—Anthony Chadwell

The Issues

The need to constantly be involved in drama, or strong emotion, is one pattern that can be very destructive in your life.

Early experience, combined with certain personality traits, sets up psycho-emotional reactions. I call these drama-loops™. They cause us to unconsciously react the same way over and over, even when it is self-defeating.

The only requirement is that we have a consistent "excuse." The excuse usually takes the form of someone to blame. It does not have to be a person; it can be a business, institution, or organization, but people are the most common.

Once the environment is right the drama-loop starts on its own accord and continues, until you are exhausted. Here is one example.

Judy

Judy feels bad about the extra weight she is carrying. In order to make herself feel better, she stops at the mall and does some shopping. She spends a few escapist hours and purchases several pieces of clothing. All this time she has a vague feeling that she is doing something wrong.

When she gets home she "surprises" her husband with a little fashion show of her new clothes. The husband, none too pleased with her purchases, does not show Judy the excitement and approval she hoped for. This lack of enthusiasm frustrates Judy. Her husband reminds her that they don't have the extra money for these clothes. He also reminds her that she was planning on losing some weight and then buying new clothes that would fit her smaller size. These reminders send her into a panic, but instead of acting out this panic, she gets angry. She brings up instances where he wasted money or bought things he did not need. She then puts all of the outfits back in the bag and tells him, in an angry tone, that she will return all of the clothes. She never really returns the clothes, but that threat is part of the drama-loop.

This entire process takes about half a day to complete, in which time Judy feels emotions ranging from elation while shopping to anger when putting the items back in the bag to "return." The loop works because Judy does not have to really be aware of anything for the entire 12-hour period.

Once she heads toward the mall, a type of unconsciousness slips over her. It all seems like a dream, or like she is acting in a movie.

When I talked to Judy the first time I was interested in the fact that she blamed her husband for all of the problems in this scenario. She was unaware that she set the loop in motion when she stopped at the mall and spent money they did not have on clothes she did not really need.

It was not until we talked, and I helped her see her part in the situation, that she realized she usually headed to the mall on days she felt fat. We began to uncover this pattern she had begun: it was usually the few days before she started her period, or after she would visit her sister, whom she envied because she was much thinner.

The need to continue initiating these drama-loops is caused by the addiction to the body chemicals that are released because of the strong emotions experienced during the cycle. The dramatic cycles are also a form of escape from anything else that the person may be experiencing at the time.

These drama-loops can be associated with weight, self-image, abandonment, jealousy, grief, gossip, or worry.

I personally have experienced this type of behavior.

My Experience

After getting divorced from my first wife, I spent a lot of time in airports, either dropping my two children off or picking them up. I always liked to get to the airport early, (a lot can go wrong getting two kids to the airport). Since we usually had time before they got on the plane, we would often share a cinnamon roll while we waited. You know the kind—warm, fresh, and full of sugar.

I did not realize it, but I had begun to eat a lot of cinnamon rolls. I ate one every few days. I noticed that I was starting to gain weight.

What was not so obvious, at first, was that I was unconsciously stopping and eating a cinnamon roll every time I started missing my children. It was an unconscious and pleasant way for me to connect with them while they were gone.

This is a minor drama-loop, but it has all of the important components. It was unconscious, had the strong emotion of grief, and I had someone to blame: my ex-wife for taking my children out of state. In my case I had the extra benefit of all that sugar acting like a drug on my system.

As I spend more time in Southern California, I have become aware of another unique drama-loop: people compulsively "dealing with their issues" (using this term in a superficial way, without actually manifesting positive change).

Rebecca

Rebecca is a very smart professional woman with two kids and a husband. I first met her when she came to see me in the clinic for back pain. As I worked to relieve the pain in her back, she told me about all of the events she was attending to help her deal with her issues.

The wide variety of groups she attended interested me. She belongs to a women's drumming circle, several support groups (including one 12-step group), several female empowerment groups, and a support group for divorced women. Of course, she was not divorced, but as she said, "someday she might be."

I had a lot of compassion for her. I was concerned about the amount of time she spent dealing with her "issues."

Rebecca spent too much time away from her home and children. Along with her busy professional life, she attended several of these events each week. Her kids were raising themselves, and her husband resented her because she was never home.

The real problem was that none of these endeavors dealt with what was really going on. Rebecca had gotten pregnant on her very first date with a man with whom she was not truly compatible. In an effort to be "good people," they had gotten married. They both resented each other and their unwanted, unplanned children.

Rebecca's drama-loop required many hours a week away from home, a frenzied drive to resolve her "issues," and anger at herself for getting pregnant and marrying a man she did not love.

These facts were obvious to me, but Rebecca was not able to hear them. The last time I spoke with her she was on her way to a fasting retreat, by herself, hoping to have a breakthrough on her issues.

Rebecca would never truly let me help her. Her drama-loop required that she stay so busy she never allowed herself to hear my suggestions. Better to take one therapeutic approach at a time and follow it wholeheartedly to its conclusion, than to jump from one idea or philosophy to another without giving it enough time or energy to impact change.

The Chadwell Method™ is an effective way to focus on one problem at a time, until real resolution can occur.

Some drama-loops can have more serious consequences, like when perpetuating some sexual torment.

Rick

Rick was enticed by "trophy" girls. Being beautiful physically was the only criteria for the women he was attracted to. I met Rick because his alcohol use had increased to the point he was not able to get to work on time and was losing income.

After our initial evaluation it became obvious that Rick had a drinking problem. In his case the drinking problem was secondary to a powerful drama-loop associated with his girlfriend.

The woman he was with tortured him in several ways. More than once she invited him over to her house on the pretext of having sex. When he arrived she'd be there with another man. This intentional manipulation would cause such a rage in Rick that he would, alternately, drink himself into oblivion, sit outside of her house, or work and watch her to make sure she was not cheating on him. This stalking behavior later became another drama-loop.

At other times she would be very sweet and loving for a few days, only to disappear for a week. Another time, after this woman drank too much at dinner, they got into an argument. On the way home she attempted to jump out of the car while it was moving. He grabbed her arm and tried to keep her in the vehicle. When they stopped at the next light, she jumped out of the car screaming. The police were called. They saw the red marks on the girl's arm, and Rick was arrested for battery. The unpredictable highs and low of the relationship kept Rick in such a state of obsessive preoccupation that he could not be present in any of the other areas of his life. Rick was participating in his own nightmare.

Rick became aware of this dangerous drama-loop but was not willing to stop it completely. He did start to attend 12-step meetings for his drinking issues. This was a good start, but he was still trying to control his relationship with this woman. The last incident he shared with me involved him getting so angry and confused, after one of these dramatic interactions, that he totaled his vehicle and was convalescing from a very serious physical injury.

Obviously Rick's case was an extreme, in that there were a tremendous number of issues involved. But his attachment to this drama-loop, having someone to blame, and the reward of escaping his day-to-day life were very significant. In the end my considered opinion would have been to refer him to a more intensive environment with in-patient care, so he could have separated himself from the triggers long enough for more healing reflection.

A lesser example of a drama-loop is Sharon.

Sharon

Sharon came into my office hoping to get some help with her headaches and breathing problems. Her intake form was filled out perfectly, and she had attached two additional typewritten sheets of "extra" information. She was very comprehensive, to say the least. Sharon was also highly verbal. She talked incessantly.

Part of the Chadwell Method is always to begin with a discovery consultation, at which the client is encouraged to share her story through a series of exploratory questions. I ask the client to tell me everything about herself she thinks is important. Sometimes clients don't quite know where to start. In this case, conversely, it was too easy for Sharon to talk about herself.

It became obvious that Sharon was very uncomfortable when she was not talking. When I politely asked her to listen to my suggestions, she could only listen for about 15 seconds. She would then burst out with more questions or more data about herself. When she stopped talking she would immediately start to fidget. Her leg would bounce up and down, or she would wring her hands.

One of the problems she complained of was not having any close friends. It was easy to see why. Her behavior acted like a barricade around her. The barrage of words had the effect of keeping people at a distance.

The tension in Sharon's nervous system so overwhelmed her, it was as if she felt she would explode if she stopped talking. Sharon was an excellent candidate for the Chadwell Method, because it provides a way for the nervous system to discard excess tension in a healthy way so that you can relax long enough to experience life differently.

These stories give some examples of how a drama-loop can play out in a person's experience. The strong emotions have a powerful drug-like effect when they are experienced. The chemical reaction in the brain is powerful enough on its own to cause the cycle to continue. In most cases there is also some other secondary gain, like in my case—a sugar buzz when eating cinnamon rolls—or Rebecca—avoiding her spouse when she did not want to be at home.

More important is that these drama-loops are acted out at an unconscious or semi-conscious level. This causes frustration and confusion. It also keeps the participant stuck in painful patterns with little chance to change.

What is more distressing is that when you are stuck in one of these loops, you never bring about any real resolution to your problems. You waste a lot of time and accomplish little in the way of lasting progress.

The Root Cause

These drama cycles originate as a way to exert control in a situation we find painful or where we feel powerless. We unconsciously repeat this action in the future when confronted with similar circumstances. This effort to feel safe works to some extent.

This is actually a constructive response to a stressful situation. The problem is that after some time, we may attempt to apply this same tactic to situations that are not appropriate.

When our strategy does not work, we do not have the ability to re-evaluate it, because it operates on an unconscious level. The result is often that we try harder and more continuously to engage in choices which are not productive.

Lack of emotional resources is another reason the drama-loops are created. It may be just that we are confronted with problems that are beyond an age appropriate level to respond. This often happens when children experience emotionally overwhelming situations.

It can also happen when we must face some trial at a point in our life when we are already exhausted or depleted for some other reason. This can occur when we are physically sick or emotionally drained. We react poorly to a problem and then the poor response becomes a habit.

A key element of these drama-loops is the need to blame someone for our distress. This fact is important. There is a strong human tendency to not take responsibility for our own lives. Having an excuse for the way we feel and act lessens the emotional pressure inside of us. This reduction in emotional pressure is very comforting and makes it easy to continue the blame game.

Last, but not to be underestimated, is the power of the neuro-chemicals created in your body by your strong emotions.

These chemicals create a self-rewarding response that makes us feel more powerful and capable. These chemicals give us a sense of well being and help us feel something like when we are in love.

Another tendency with many people that perpetuates these cycles is when we are too absorbed in our own selfish and limited desires. Your wants and your needs become all you think about. This form of egotism puts us at the center of the universe and warps our sense of self-importance. Whatever we think about becomes bigger, at least in our own minds.

From this standpoint it seems logical to be consumed with what makes us happy. Unfortunately, this viewpoint only causes isolation and pain. Few people are willing to be around someone who is so self—engrossed. It is too draining.

You know that this applies to you if you need to be the center of attention in a social setting, or if, when you meet someone, you immediately begin talking about yourself rather than listening to what that person has to say.

The Solution

These drama-loops are an attempt to fix a problem by way of subconscious avoidance of the real issue.

In the case of Judy, had she spent the time, effort, and money on losing weight and living a healthy lifestyle, she would not have needed to participate in the drama-loop of shopping and "returning."

If Rick had developed the skills to look for a woman who had more to offer than just physical beauty, he may have been able to find a person who could have provided the security and companionship he really wanted.

The saying "it is hard to wash your clothes while you are wearing them" is very true with these dysfunctional cycles. When you first realize you are blaming someone and that they have become part of your drama-loop, try to stay away from them if at all possible.

You can do this by giving yourself a "time-out." This period of separation includes no talking, texting, e-mails, or phone calls. Also, no relaying of messages by using another person. If it is possible let the other person know what you are doing and why. This is not always realistic because of the nature of the drama-loop. Often the process of asking for alone time can become a ploy that just continues the cycle.

It is mandatory to avoid the person or people so that you can gain some objectivity. Then find a quiet place for reflection, and write down all of the parts of the drama that come to mind.

You may need some help from someone you trust that has no secondary gain by helping you. For example, don't ask a man who is attracted to you to help you understand the cycle about another man. That is secondary gain, because he is in a position to manipulate you.

After you feel like you have a good sense of all the parts to your cycle, see what you are really looking for. For example, do you really want love, companionship, money, or sex? Be honest, and then see if there is a less dramatic way to obtain what you really want.

You may initially go through a type of withdrawal, just like withdrawal from many drugs. You may feel worse for a while because of the vacuum created by not filling your day with drama.

Fill this time in by doing something that gets you "out of yourself" in a positive and healthy way; no drugs alcohol, promiscuous sex, or anything else that is itself addicting.

Try watching happy movies or taking a class on something that has always interested you but you never made time for. Go dancing with friends or listen to uplifting music. If you have not been to church for a long time, go back and look at that option with new eyes. The list of positive alternatives is endless, but you may need to put a lot of effort into finding something constructive in the beginning. Be careful you are not just doing an activity that will put you in an environment to meet the next "Mr. or Ms. Wrong." Doing this is simply another distraction! Give yourself time to change.

Gradually you will feel better, and the self-esteem that is gained from behaving differently will become very satisfying.

If your situation is more extreme I often suggest this solution: in order to find the answer to your drama-loop, you may first need to take a vacation from your day-to-day world. This can happen an hour at a time in therapy, or as I often suggest, by taking a "silent sabbatical" and "media fast."

I usually suggest taking two days away from your life as usual. A weekend works great. Let everyone know you will not be available *for any reason*. This means you *do not talk* for two full days. It is also mandatory that you have no contact with your normal world.

No television, reading, e-mail, or computers. Plan accordingly so that you will not be distracted. Just be alone with yourself. This experiment is often the first time a person has ever been alone without distraction in his entire life. It can be very scary. Pick a place away from your home. There are retreat centers all over the country that specialize in providing a safe location that is isolated from the world. I particularly like renting a small cabin up in Big Bear, California. If possible make it far enough away from your home that you feel like you are in another world, apart from your typical daily life.

One thing you can do during these two days is write. Write about whatever comes into your mind, whatever seems important. This process can be very enlightening.

The other thing you can do is pray. Prayer is a direct link between you and something more wise and powerful than yourself. For some, meditation can be an answer. There are all types of meditation. One of my favorites is to sit comfortably with my spine straight and simply count my inhalations 1 to 10. When you get to 10, start over. Prayer and meditation are two powerful ways to change your nervous system and slow your thoughts. Try it!

During this unique period, you may actually find out what is really important to you. You may also realize how much of your life you have been wasting on useless desires and blaming other people.

Hopefully you will re-emerge with a new plan and an awareness of what is really necessary for you to be happy.

Key Ideas to Remember

- Physically separate yourself from the person(s) involved in creating the drama-loop.
- You are only aware of the pain caused by the drama-loop.
- The actual drama-loop is unconscious.
- You may need help mapping out or "uncovering" the cycle.
- This discovery process must be done in solitude.
- Find what you really need.
- Learn new and healthy ways to get that need met.

Chapter 6:

Early Trauma Still With You

**"Parents are not the cause, merely the
continuation of a cycle."**
-Anthony Chadwell

The Issues

Trauma is much more common than most people are aware. The more people I have worked with in my practice, the more I have learned that time and again a high percentage of clients' lives are strongly impacted by traumatic events which occurred in their childhoods or early adult lives. The trauma these people experience directly affects the quality of their personal relationships as well as their own relationship with the world around them.

Trauma means any event or situation that overwhelms a person's emotional, physical, or spiritual capacity at the time it occurred. This is much more likely with children, of course, because these characteristics of their humanity are not yet fully developed and are therefore more vulnerable.

When confronted by a situation that overwhelms us, it puts a shock or strain in our system, like sending too much electrical current into an electronic device, and it overloads the circuits. Humans are provided with an amazing body, mind, and soul capable of adapting to this shock.

As I mentioned earlier, I call this adapting response a traumatic emotional overlay™. This adaptation is very important for our survival: it allows us to continue to function by "cutting off" or altering parts of our true selves. This alteration of our true self affects our personality, often by limiting our ability to express who we really are. If this adaptation is not recognized and treated, it becomes a permanent part of our life.

These traumatic emotional overlays may get lodged in the physical, mental, emotional, or spiritual level of our bodies. For example, one man who came to see me had a father who beat him so severely and frequently that he ceased to cry during these abusive episodes. He felt the only way he could survive (and retaliate) in this horrible situation was to not let his father see that the beating had any effect on him. So he stopped crying completely. That normal physical/emotional response was disconnected by the trauma he endured.

This man had become successful in many ways by the time I saw him. Yet his traumatic emotional overlay had grown until he had actually stopped expressing *any* emotion that he felt made him vulnerable in any way. He was unable to have close associations with people. All people were just too threatening for him, due to this early childhood abuse. He wanted to have an intimate relationship with a woman, but the women he would meet would quickly experience how emotionally unavailable he was. They would rarely accept a second date with him. He didn't know how to open up.

Traumatic emotional overlays also affect our cognitive ability, our ability to think and to solve problems. Trauma puts us in another world, a world that is different from the one we lived in before the trauma. Prior to the overwhelming experience we may have felt safe. We may have felt like there was some order or trustworthiness to our lives. The traumatic experience shakes the foundation of our reality, and we may subsequently process the information delivered to our brain by the five senses in a different way, often feeling scared and confused as a result. Doing simple tasks that should be easy becomes very difficult.

I disclosed earlier how a physical trauma to my head from a vehicle accident had hindered me from solving mathematic problems. Balancing my checkbook was difficult; trying to figure out which cell phone plan I needed was impossible! The part of my brain that processed abstract concepts, like mathematics and spatial relationships, had been diminished. As a result of the previous accident impact, my neuro-processing ability had been disrupted.

Lori

Lori came to see me because of her compulsive behavior. She had seen her father's body a few minutes after he had committed suicide. It was a horrific experience for her. In that one moment, that one experience, she lost touch with anything that made her feel safe in the world.

Her father died when she was sixteen years old. I saw Lori in her mid-twenties. She had suffered for ten years from various compulsions to "stay safe." She would continually check to see if the front door was locked. Before she went to bed at night, she would brace a chair under the bedroom doorknob to prevent someone from coming in while she slept. Often, after she was in bed she would remind herself how "crazy" this habit was. She would get out of bed, remove the chair, and get back in bed. Within 5 minutes an emotional-mental battle would ensue, and she would again get out of bed to prop the chair under the door. This cycle might repeat itself 20 or 30 times before Lori would finally succumb to sleep.

This traumatic emotional overlay would cause Lori to have panic attacks every day prior to taking a shower. She could not stand to be contained or "surrounded." When she was in the shower with the water running, Lori knew she could not hear if someone was breaking into her home. She felt very vulnerable all of the time. In a very real sense, her capacity to enjoy life had left her after the shock of her father's death at his own hand.

Lori is a textbook example of how traumatic events can change the world in which we live, (or more to the point, change how we respond to the world around us). A bit of natural caution toward "the unknown" is normal and healthy. However, when you have trouble navigating very simple basics of living peacefully, with joy and anticipation, you must try to isolate the cause(s) before healing can begin.

Mentally, physically, and emotionally trauma may also steal our capacity to see our lives in a larger spiritual context.

Harry

Harry had come to see me after learning that bodywork and cranial therapy were a quick and efficient way to release trauma from the body. Harry had been educated at a religious boarding school. As part of a building expansion program at the school, he and a bunch of other boys were forced to move a graveyard. They were forced to dig up old decaying coffins and bodies, carry them to a new location, and then re-bury them. Many of the bodies were infants and children.

The effect of this terrifying and overwhelming experience was devastating to him. The mind of this young man was simply not capable of handling such a stressful situation at that age. All at once, he was confronted with death, the death of other children and, of course, his own mortality and inevitable death. He was also confused about how the church leadership, who professed to love him, could put him and his fellow students in such an agonizing and psychologically damaging situation. A tremendous conflict developed within Harry. How could life be this way? Why does God let children die? What is going to happen when I die one day? How can God love us and allow this to happen?

Feeling he had no safe place to turn for answers, Harry simply buried this stressful trauma deep in the recesses of his soul and vowed that he would never think about it again.

This plan worked for several years. The problem with stored traumatic emotional overlays is something akin to when someone tries to hold a volleyball under water: it can be done as long as that is all you do! Eventually, the trauma finds a way out to the surface. It can be through depression, anger, or any form of addictive behavior.

I believe we are given the opportunity to resolve these traumatic emotional overlays when we have enough resources available to start to resolve them. The resources include several things:

- Someone to help and guide us
- A safe environment to express ourselves without judgment
- Most important, willingness
- Resources of time and or money.

Harry continued to have loathing for the religious organization that was associated with the school, and a distrust of any God who would put him in this position in the first place. However, after several treatments at my Center, his body was able to let go of most of the shock that had kept him emotionally tortured, angry, and shut down for years.

With traumatic emotional overlays we get stuck in a survival mode. We may just exist without really being able to live fully. We may feel "dull," lack interest in new experiences, and over—or under-react to day-to-day stresses.

Obviously, the degrees of trauma, and its effect on us as individuals, range enormously. In my own story in the early part of this book I talked about leaving the security of my grandparents' home as a child and moving to a big city. For me, at that time, the experience was traumatic. For someone else, under different circumstances, this could easily have been a great adventure.

My example is minor compared to experiences other people have had, but it brings up two important points.

1. Trauma encompasses a range of events, from slight deprivation or overindulgence in some area, to extreme emotional, physical, spiritual, and sexual abuse.
2. The context or environment in which the trauma takes place, and the *capacity of the individual at that time*, determine the extent to which the person will be affected by the incident. This includes state of mind, general physical health, prior accidents, or previous trauma.

Bill

Bill was a pilot in World War II. His plane was shot down over Germany. As he careened toward Earth and was about to hit the ground, he was sure he was going to die. Bill came to, surrounded by a bunch of angry local German citizens. They beat and imprisoned him and held him for days, waiting for the German military authorities to come get him.

Bill told me his story and said he was "aware of the miracle of escaping the crashed plane" and was filled with a sense of love and awe. He was amazed he was still alive! Even as the scared citizens beat him, he said, "I felt a sense of understanding and compassion for them."

Bill was able to escape and eventually got back to America. When I met him he was in his seventies. He had retained his loving benevolence all of these years, a fascinating man, full of life, love and compassion. One only needed to be around Bill for a few minutes to sense that he had discovered something important: his love for other people and an ability to stay detached from circumstances.

Bill's story is interesting and inspirational, because obviously he had experienced major trauma: being shot-down, a plane crash, intense fear, being beaten, being imprisoned, and escaping. How is it that Bill, by his own admission, was changed for the better by this catastrophic experience?

This is a good example of how the individual person and the environment alter the response to the trauma.

Bill was at war. He had joined the Air Force willingly, convinced he was fighting for an important and just cause, as most young men did during World War II. The feeling that he was doing something right and important gave him a reason to be in that situation, and *it was his choice*. Bill also had grown up with a set of spiritual beliefs, Catholicism, which provided him with a concept of God. He had some faith. That faith grew stronger after his plane was shot down.

Not only was Bill able to survive what we would all know as trauma, he was able to use that experience to actually thrive.

You can see from these few examples that traumatic experiences enter our lives in a variety of ways and have different impacts on us, based on our particular personalities and circumstances. I use the example of Bill to show how adaptable we can be when our bodies are healthy and our attitudes are optimistic and grateful.

The Root Cause

Trauma takes away our feelings of positive self esteem and safety. It makes us feel "less than" other people. When we feel unworthy, or damaged in some way, we may lower our standards and associate with people who are not good for us. We "settle" for people and conditions that hurt us or do not have our best interests at heart. These unhealthy relationships perpetuate the traumatic emotional overlay.

Let's look at some more common examples of how we can experience trauma.

Divorce

Divorce is a very common form of traumatic experience in our culture. Virtually every client I work with, who came from parents who divorced, acknowledges that their parents' divorce was a major damaging event in their lives.

Let us consider the situation from the viewpoint of a child whose parents are getting a divorce. The divorce environment is often very stressful and toxic. A child may absorb any number of overwhelming traumatic emotional overlays during this time, which can potentially cause problems later in his adult relationships.

A child may feel the deep loss of the family and home life with which he was familiar. He may feel betrayed by one or both parents for what he perceives as their part in the divorce. He may feel a general confusion about his future, about where and with whom he will live. These stresses can affect him at a very basic survival level. After all, parents are perceived to be protectors of us as children. The loss of the familiar relationship with his parents may even feel life-threatening.

If the divorce is a very hostile and angry one, the child may absorb this anger into his emotional energy field. This highly charged emotional environment might create a change in the child's normal emotional range, forcing him to become permanently "locked" into anger or fear with no safe place to resolve it.

Parents often use the child as a pawn or a bargaining chip to punish or extort the other parent. This power struggle may crush the child's ability to feel safe with either parent after the divorce. Contrarily, the child may feel empowered by being put in the middle of the fight and learn to use this opportunity as a way to manipulate the parents for things he wants. This is especially true materially.

The child may be put in a no-win situation. Young children in particular are subject to trauma when forced to "choose" which parent they want to live with, or even worse, forced to legally testify against one parent.

If the two parents live in separate houses or towns the child is forced to learn to live in two different worlds. The two homes may have different sets of rules. Children often learn to be secretive, keeping certain facts from one parent, because the other parent has instructed them to do so. It is easy for these children to learn to tell lies for their own advantage. These patterns often carry on in their later adult relations creating more traumatic dysfunction. These dysfunctions are self-perpetuating.

Once a child is exposed to the conflicts and drama involved in a divorce, his future relationships will tend to follow the same pattern. These patterns tend to re-create themselves generation after generation, unless real work is done to break the cycle. Divorce creates a breeding-ground for many forms of traumatic dysfunction.

Alcohol and Other Drugs

Drugs and alcohol are another culprit in creating disruption and trauma of all types in a child. At this point, we will learn how children are affected by their parents' use of mood-altering substances. Later in the book we will discuss at length the relationship that develops between the user and her drug of choice.

Children who are exposed to parents who drink regularly to the point that their personality and thinking change to a noticeable degree are in an environment that can lead to traumatic emotional overlays. The common misconception that a parent or guardian must drink heavily, often, or be falling-down-drunk in order to negatively affect the child is just that—a misconception, and it is incorrect.

Even in households where one or both parents drink moderately in order to change their feelings or manage stress, an unhealthy pattern can be set for the child who is exposed to it. The child may not have a healthy example of how to manage normal life stressors in a constructive way. As adults they are likely to use alcohol, marijuana, or other substances as a means of escape and to cope in the same way.

In homes where alcohol or any other drug is used heavily, the likelihood of traumatic emotional overlays, both physical and emotional, increases tremendously. Homes in which substances are abused create an unstable environment for the child to develop. The parents' inconsistent moods and personalities, because of substance use, adds to this instability. This dysfunction may be made worse in homes stricken with poverty, where the basics of food and shelter are absent.

A child quickly learns to mask feelings and hide information in order to exist and "survive" in a toxic home. He may also learn to keep secrets from one or the other parent in order to keep the household from exploding. He learns to "time" certain behaviors, until the parent is in a "good mood" (for example, waiting to ask a parent for money until after he has had a few drinks, or staying away from the house when the parent is hung-over). An unstable environment causes an overlay of traumatic fear in a child; that trauma then carries on into later relationships because his emotional response to current circumstances is not appropriate.

Children in a divorce situation often over-bond with one or the other parent in order to feel safe. They may bond with the drinker in order to be "one of the guys," or with the non-drinking spouse as a surrogate mate to help "take care of the family" or be "momma's big man." This inappropriate bonding leads to relationship confusion. For example, when a man is overly bonded to his mother as a child, this pattern may continue after he is married, when he should be making his wife his main relationship priority. A woman who remains "daddy's little girl" after she is old enough to be emotionally and financially self-reliant also finds relationships difficult. She may depend on her father for needs that should be fulfilled by her husband.

If the addiction is severe enough, the child may be forced to take on adult roles and activities too early in his life. He may need to start working to contribute to the family's finances when he is at an age at which he should be finishing school. He may be forced to be a "parent" to his younger siblings because the actual parents are not available due to their substance (or emotional) abuse, or he may be put in a position to need to lie to cover for his parents' irresponsibility.

We have talked about two very common situations that are likely to create a traumatic emotional overlay onto the energy field of a child. The list of the possible ways trauma can be experienced is very long.

Anytime children experience *or* witness violence to *any* degree there is likely to be a traumatic emotional overlay. This may include vehicle accidents, family fighting, or criminal violence.

Children or young people who are involved in natural disasters like earthquakes or floods can be traumatized. I remember when I was about 10 years old being in a house that was hit by a flash flood. For years after that anytime storm clouds would gather my heart would start racing, and I would feel panicky. This is a traumatic emotional overlay created when I felt powerless over the flooding water.

Some traumatic emotional overlays are caused not by events taking place, but rather by something *not* happening. Neglect is one of those examples. Neglect can also happen on the physical, mental, emotional, or spiritual level.

When someone is denied a basic need, something mandatory for proper development, a trauma may occur. If someone does not have enough food, safe shelter, loving support, encouragement, or education, an elusive emotional wound may be experienced. The emotional overlay from neglect has the same effect in relationship development, although perhaps in a lesser form than the more obvious inflicted traumas we outlined earlier. Children that experience neglect may perpetuate that traumatic emotional overlay by living in poverty or by becoming miserly, hoarding objects or money beyond what is practical in order to create a sense of security.

Overindulgence: The Opposite End of the Spectrum

Up to this point we have been describing negative events that happen *to* us that are by nature traumatizing. *Having too much can cause as much harm as having too little.* In order to really understand the extent to which traumatic emotional overlays may occur in quite contrary circumstances, let's discuss a situation that causes the same type of trauma in a different way.

Children who are raised in an atmosphere that supports them in a balanced and loving way usually thrive and grow to carry that balanced way of living into their own lives and families. Children who are overindulged often end up struggling with anger, depression, or some other trouble because they have an overinflated sense of self-importance.

Overindulgence-caused traumatic emotional overlays are created when a child or young person receives out of proportion to what they give. As an infant, a baby is helpless and must be taken care of. As a child grows, his responsibility should also grow according to his ability. It is important to gain the perspective that we are not the center of the universe, and the world is composed of other people who also have a right to have their needs met.

Like most of my generation, when I was growing up it was common in my neighborhood for children to have "chores." Chores were tasks that children performed according to their age and ability. The reward was usually an "allowance" or some privilege, like going to the movies, or staying up a little later than usual. If we wanted extra money we figured out a way to earn it.

I often meet children in my clinic who are not required to do anything around the house. Someone is hired to mow the grass, clean the pool, and often keep the house clean. These children are bored with everything. They are lethargic and unmotivated. We all need to learn to be responsible, and the earlier that is experienced in a positive way, the better. Without having some age-appropriate responsibilities, children do not learn normal self esteem. Positive self esteem leads to a fundamental sense of self-worth. A parent's job is to raise a child that is educated, independent, and self-reliant.

Carmen

Carmen's mother brought her in to see me because she was moody and would not focus enough to get her schoolwork done. Carmen was 15 but carried herself like a mature woman. She came from an affluent family. Her father traveled extensively, and her mother was always the "bad guy" around the house, trying to discipline and raise the children almost as a single parent. Her mother was trying to "keep the peace" and at the same time make up for her father's continual absence.

After her mother left the room, Carmen took on another personality, she softened and started to act and speak in a way that was more age appropriate. Carmen was not required to do anything except go to school. If she whined about going, her mother would bribe her with new clothes. If she wanted to stay up until 2 AM and talk or text on her phone, her mother would let her. She had extreme mood swings that she blamed on her hormones and menstrual cycle. She spoke disrespectfully to her parents and her sibling.

Carmen's traumatic emotional overlay was caused by overindulgence. She had been spoiled, and even more importantly, she was fully aware of it. She acknowledged to me that she consciously punished her parents, that she really did not have hormonal mood swings, and that she was angry all of the time.

Carmen is an example of someone who is suffering from too much indulgence. She has no structure or rules to guide her emotional growth. She has been given the authority role in her house, instead of her parents being the authority, and she is suffering as a result of it. When Carmen leaves her parents' home, she will likely attract men who treat her the same way, and in the same way, she will resent and disrespect them, as she now does her parents.

We all need to experience the consequences of our actions, good and bad. If we are deprived of this normal learning experience as children, it is very difficult to learn as an adult. It can be done, but it usually requires a lot of awareness and willingness to grow in order to see our own part in the problems we have created.

The Solution

Traumatic emotional overlays get blocked at a very deep level in your body, and their effects are widespread, influencing almost every area of your life. If you want to develop healthier relationships with other people, you need to be as healthy as possible first.

The change required to grow past these traumas must take place at an equally deep level for it to be effective and permanent. I have found very few people have been able to recover on their own. It is best to have help throughout the healing process. Support of a loving and understanding person speeds the process and keeps the subject from feeling overwhelmed.

Talk therapy can be useful in the early phases of healing. This is the time in recovery when you must mature to a point, become aware that something is wrong, and start to become willing to do something about the problems with which you are presented.

During this time you can look back to analyze what happened and how you have been changed as a result of prior experiences. Having someone to talk with allows you to crystalize all of the conflicting thoughts and feelings. It is a time to write and get the memories out on paper, so that you can look at them objectively.

A healthy body speeds the process of recovery. Your body needs proper nutrition, water, exercise, and rest to operate efficiently. If you have let your health decline, *now* is the time to change that.

Every thought creates a series of chemicals that flood the body. You can confirm this for yourself. Have you ever noticed, when a police car pulls behind you, how your heart rate goes up? That is adrenaline being pumped into your blood stream. The same type of chemical reaction occurs in a similar way with *every* thought you think. Joyful thoughts create joyful chemicals, stressful thoughts create stressful chemicals, and angry thoughts create angry chemicals. This phenomenon is why you can look at someone and get a general idea of their predominant thought pattern: the chemistry shows in the body, especially the face.

One type of chemical that is altered by traumatic emotional overlays are hormones. It is very important to do the work necessary to balance your hormones during recovery from trauma. Your hormones may have been adversely affected for years because of the stress you experienced.

Regular exercise is also very important, to keep your lungs clear and your blood pure. Exercise also adds a general sense of well-being that makes recovery easier.

Bodywork and cranial therapy are the most effective way to release traumatic emotional overlays, especially after some talk therapy has been utilized to uncover the basic concerns. Time and time again I have witnessed people change almost overnight by releasing trauma with bodywork and cranial therapy. This type of therapy actually gets to the same energetic level as the trauma. What is held in the body can be released permanently in this way.

This type of energetic work does not move the bones around, nor is it massage. It is a hands-on modality that releases the energetic blocks that a person is carrying. A professional, ethical, and well-trained therapist whose intentions are pure helps to achieve the desired outcomes. A subject must really be able to trust the person with whom she is working. The relationship between the subject and the therapist needs to be safe and professional at all times. You need to be able to ask questions and to guide the treatment session as you feel appropriate. The therapist must provide a safe environment that allows your body to heal itself. No physical or emotional force should be used. The body already has the perfect plan for your healing. A good therapist supports your body by allowing that perfection to manifest.

When therapy is applied in this way the body controls the rate of healing. With this approach you are not negatively affected by the treatment, and the results are more permanent.

Bodywork and cranial therapy are important types of treatments that allow "open space" in your body. This space is an emotional and energetic release or "unwinding." It feels great! After only the first session, many clients comment that this is the most relaxed they have felt in years, or that they feel blissful. This "space" is what allows for new ideas and information to penetrate us. It allows *love* and *grace* to come into our lives.

One of the ways we know we are healing the traumatic emotional overlay is that we become willing to forgive. Many people make a conscious or unconscious vow that they will not forgive someone who has hurt them in the past. This may be especially true of people who injured you physically. Ironically, this defiance is what further harms you. It is like a chain that binds you to a past traumatic person or event. Until you choose to forgive, you will never be fully healed.

This forgiveness must also include you. Very often after being a victim of some type of trauma, you perpetuate the cycle by continuing to victimize yourself with negative thoughts and actions. After time the original trauma may be insignificant compared to what you have done to harm yourself!

After you have done the work necessary to resolve your traumatic emotional overlays, be willing to share your experience with other people. If you have been fortunate enough to seek and find a way to free yourself from prior traumas and have begun to build healthier, happier relationships in your life, let other people know how you did it. As I said in the very beginning, a tremendous number of people suffer from traumatic emotional overlays of various types. You are in a unique position to help them. Do it!

Remember, help is best given by someone who has overcome his or her own difficulties, not in theory but in reality. You will know you have succeeded when you are aware that you have forgiven every person involved with your traumatic emotional overlay, including yourself.

Key Ideas to Remember

- Make a written list of past traumas.
- Find a practitioner you trust to support you during this healing process, and start receiving regular energetic bodywork and/or cranial therapy.
- Remember you are only as sick as your secrets.
- Maintain a generally healthy body with diet, nutrition, exercise and rest.
- Use the "space" created with this therapy to forgive everyone and every situation that has negatively affected you.
- Consider journaling as part of your therapy.
- *After* you have fully resolved your own traumatic emotional overlays, share your success and hope with others.

Chapter 7:

Substances—Relationship With Feeling Different

"You can never stop a bad habit; you can only replace it with a better one."
-Anthony Chadwell

The Issues

Many situations cause us to feel uncomfortable. We humans are incredibly inventive in finding relief from the stress we feel. One of the most effective ways to change the way we feel is by using various mood-or mind-altering substances.

In this chapter I am going to use the words alcohol and drugs interchangeably, but I want to be clear: I am talking about *any* substance or activity that brings about a change in the way we feel. This includes alcohol, recreational and prescription drugs, food, overeating, under eating, obsessing about what you eat, sex in all forms, pornography, masturbation, internet shopping, gambling, compulsive exercise, and the list goes on and on.

You get the idea? We have a myriad of ways to change the way we feel. Applied reasonably, these options can be healthy. Used to excess, these options can cause more problems than they solve.

All of these actions cause us to feel temporarily different. These activities create a change in the neurochemistry in our brains. It is this change in chemistry that makes us feel relaxed or stimulated, as the case may be. It is the same with alcohol. It acts on our body to make us feel relaxed after having one or two drinks. If we continue to consume large quantities of alcohol, we are no longer relaxed; we are poisoned. It is this over-intoxicated poisoning that leads to bad behaviors, like driving a vehicle while under the influence, or in extreme cases "blacking out" or "passing out" completely.

Over time, using substance to change the way we feel can become a pattern. If the pattern continues it becomes a habit. If the habit continues it may become an addiction. Addictions, in the final phases, often lead to physical death.

When someone starts to get involved with this habit of escaping, they start to form a relationship with the alcohol. As the relationship with alcohol continues, it can become the person's primary relationship. When your primary relationship is with alcohol, it is necessary to make other relationships less important.

Kenny

Kenny started his drug use as many people do by smoking some pot with his friends when he was 13 or 14 years old. He was good-looking, charming, funny and very outgoing. People liked Kenny and they liked to be around him. Kenny's parents' garage became the cool neighborhood place to go after school. His parents were never home, and someone usually had some marijuana. Everyone had a good time.

Eventually Kenny started to buy larger qualities of pot and then started to sell it to his friends in smaller amounts for a profit. This dealing became a source of income for Kenny. Within a year Kenny started to use various pills, and since he had a ready-made network of clients, he started to sell pills as well as marijuana.

After graduation Kenny made an arrangement with his parents to remodel the garage and turn it into an apartment. It was frequented by a lot of people coming and going, just saying hello or buying whatever drugs Kenny had that day.

Kenny was eventually arrested for dealing drugs, and as a condition of his parole went into a drug treatment facility. After his release he returned home to his parents' garage-apartment and stayed drug-free for 9 months. Kenny started to exercise regularly, but the underlying issues that had allowed his original drug problem to flourish were never addressed.

I met Kenny in his late twenties. He was enormous, not from fat, but from muscle. At a glance it was obvious that Kenny was using steroids. The funny and outgoing adolescent had been replaced with a very serious and unhappy man. Kenny was isolated, and the only physical contact he had were the superficial conversations with other people at the gym, while he was working out.

Kenny was never willing to go into treatment for his steroid abuse, and the last I heard he had died from a heart attack while mowing his mother's front yard.

This is a sad example of the progressive path of untreated addiction. Kenny had no idea in those early days of smoking pot that he would eventually die as a result of drug abuse.

People are multidimensional, and addiction can occur within any or all of these dimensions.

Mental Level

Life presents us with a series of challenges that must be overcome. The process of thinking about and creating strategies to conquer these challenges bring about mental pressure. For some people this pressure is exhilarating and very enjoyable. For others this mental pressure may be perceived as either uncomfortable or unbearable. If the activities of life are felt on the higher end of the spectrum, it is not uncommon for a person having these extreme sensations to try to avoid them or escape these feelings all together.

Substances are a good way to do this. To a point, they can be useful as a temporary way to handle a situation. The problem is that the challenges of life continue to occur. That is the nature of life. The old adage, "'What do you get after you successfully pass a life-challenge?' Answer: 'A bigger challenge,'" is most often true!

Two things happen when we rely on a substance to alleviate the mental pressure we feel:

1. We never build the emotional agility to handle life's problems without being under the influence of a substance.
2. By using a substance, we often create more problems.

A simple example is that it is much easier to pay your power bill when it is due rather than after the power company has shut off your electricity. Along the way it is easier to pay it late than not at all. And it is easier to negotiate a payment plan with the power company than to pay the fees and put up with the aggravation of having your power turned off, only to have the chore of getting it turned back on again.

People who have a strong relationship with alcohol eventually have a lot of problems like this. They avoid dealing effectively with people and situations as they develop, and as a result circumstances become more complicated.

Emotional Level

Emotional immaturity and vulnerability occur for many reasons. When we are unable to respond to real life situations in a healthy way, because of our sense of insecurity or low self-worth, a defensive response may be activated. To offset this emotional vulnerability alcohol is often used to create a synthetic sense of safety, a chemical cocoon that protects us against the outside world.

When someone uses alcohol or drugs to create this false security he is forced to rely on this coping mechanism more and more. He also falls into the pattern of not developing the necessary emotional skill to deal with life successfully without drugs.

He is often immature, selfish, and inconsiderate of the people around him. He wants to be taken care of and then resents the people who help him. He insists he can "do it himself" when in reality he has not built the necessary emotional muscle to function independently.

As his relationship with alcohol continues, the difference between his emotional age and his biological age widens. In a very real way growth stops when alcohol is used, because it interrupts brain development. It is not uncommon to see a 40-year-old woman talk and respond to stress like a 15-year-old girl. As this process continues, the person becomes more and more isolated. This isolation hinders her from developing relationships with other people. If treatment is not sought, the end result can be tragic.

Physical Level

The use of alcohol and other drugs can cause real physical dependence leading to death if abruptly discontinued. The body learns to function with the drug in the system, and if not available the body can have a severe reaction to its discontinuation. Acute detoxification from drugs and alcohol should always be conducted in a medical facility capable of handling this potentially critical situation.

The fact that all drugs lead to tolerance needs to be considered. Tolerance means that more and more of a substance is required to have the same effect. If the tolerance is allowed to become too high, then the amount of the drug can actually kill the person before its euphoric effect can be felt. This sometimes happens when a person is released from a detox setting and immediately returns to using. If he returns to the amount that he used prior to detox, it can cause his death. His tolerance was lowered by temporarily not having the drug in his system.

Spiritual Level

A relationship with a substance that progresses to an extreme has an effect on the spiritual level. When we use a substance for too long a time, or in too large a quantity, it literally put us in another reality. It becomes a spiritual disease (dis-ease) destroying us from the inside out.

We can feel like there is no God, or that God has abandoned us. Of course this is not true. This feeling is a by-product of the disease of addiction. Addicts feel they are living in "hell" and that there is no hope for them. They really feel their situation will never change; they often reach a point of hopelessness.

If this is allowed to continue without intervention or treatment, they will end up in prison, a hospital or psychiatric facility, or ultimately dying as a result of this untreated state.

There are many stories about jail-house conversions. When a person finally ends up in jail or some other institution, he may hit a "bottom." At the very point he feels the lowest, he pauses and ask God for help. I have meet many people who have experienced some form of this phenomenon. Without exception they report feeling as if "something" inside of them changed. What is more important is that they behave, live, and act differently afterwards. It is a real spiritual experience.

There are few things more frustrating than watching someone you care about agonizing with an out-of-control relationship with substances. Until the person hits a "bottom" of some sort, or until an intervention gives them a period of time to detox and experience life without the drug, it is unlikely they will be able to muster the willingness to seek treatment and recovery on a permanent basis. Often these approaches need to be repeated several times until life and death experience shatters the person's delusive existence and provides him with the desire to seek help.

The Root Cause

Under all addiction is the desire to be whole. Ultimately we have an innate desire to be complete, and substances temporarily give us that feeling. One of the terms for alcohol is "spirits." We are trying to fill up our spiritual essence with a spirit that is outside of us, instead of coming into a relationship with and enhancing our own true spiritual natures.

One of the temptations of using external spirits like alcohol is that it is an extremely easy way to change the way we feel. It does not take much effort to pour a drink, drink it, and feel the immediate result.

My Experience

I was in my early 30s when I first started having migraine headaches. It was normal for the doctors I visited to prescribe painkillers for my condition. Since I have an addictive personality, it was also normal for me to take them, lots of them.

As my tolerance increased so did the number of pills I took each day. The relaxing, euphoric effect I received from the pills made it very easy not *to look at the situations in my life that had caused the headaches in the first place. My marriage was less than perfect, my diet was very poor, and I was overwhelmed and stressed running a business that had grown beyond my capability to manage.*

No wonder I liked the pills! It was much easier to take a few pills than to make the difficult but necessary changes to balance my life.

There are other dynamics that underlie the use of alcohol and its ability to help us escape the fear and boredom of day-to-day life. This **escapist** tendency has rewards that reach beyond just the use of alcohol. Avoidance of growth has its own rewards—*for a time*. Occasionally, paradoxically to what I said before, this escapist behavior has a beneficial effect: it gives us time to mature inwardly without the dealing with the stresses of life. It is like taking a break from living for a time.

However, it is better to restructure and simplify the duties of life *without* alcohol when possible, rather than using a chemical to create a synthetic existence. If we temporarily create a simple and safe environment in which to grow, we will later be in a much better state of mind to re-enter our mainstream life.

Isolation is another by-product of substance use. While using substances our behavior may become erratic. People who abuse substances eventually isolate to protect themselves from the reflection of their behavior as shown to them by other people's reactions. Isolation allows the user to continue to use, unimpeded by others' judgments or other conflicts.

Anger can also be avoided by the use of alcohol and drugs. Some people use alcohol as a way to manage their continuously angry state of mind. When someone has adopted the state of mind of being angry or enraged all of the time, substances can help her cope in a way that is less destructive than acting-out the anger she feels physically toward other people, or inwardly toward herself. Alcohol acts as a pressure relief valve.

Self pity is another common emotional state that attracts the use of drugs. Self pity develops when an emotionally immature person feels that life has cheeted her in some way. She feels that she is "owed" more than she is receiving. The emotional immaturity that causes these strong feelings can be temporarily concealed by using drugs or engaging in other mood-altering actions.

The effort to grow spiritually takes a sizeable and consistent effort. We can delay our personal growth by using drugs and alcohol, but it is only a temporary delay. Eventually we will be forced by life's circumstances to apply the effort required to grow past the point of using any substance to numb us or in any way hinder our naturally maturing growth.

The Solution

Physical Recovery

The solution to addiction needs to specifically address the area in which the addiction primarily resides. Addiction can affect any or all of the areas of your life—physical, mental, emotional, or spiritual. It is very difficult to make any positive emotional change when the physical body is full of toxic by-products from drug use. This fact becomes obvious to anyone who has experienced a hangover.

When you wake up with a hangover you feel sick, tired, and confused. You lack energy; getting to work is an effort, and your productivity suffers. For those who use alcohol frequently or daily, this state becomes "normal" for them. Your body adapts to the poison.

The first step toward any hope of real recovery is detoxification. If the addiction is serious enough, it must be done in a medical setting. Anyone who has chemical toxicity needs to make an effort to clean out his body.

Start with your digestion. Drink a lot of water, a minimum of one ounce for every two pounds of body weight per day.

It is imperative that you eat a nutritious diet. If you have been using substances for a long time, it is likely that your nutritional storehouse is depleted. Start by eating mostly vegetables. The closer to the raw state, the better. If need be lightly steam or stir-fry for a different taste.

Add some protein in the form of lean meats, eggs, or a good quality protein drink. Eat some fresh fruit every day. The people I have put on an optimal diet and nutritional health plan have very few drug or alcohol cravings after they stop using, simply because they are getting all of the nutrition they need. Proper nutrition helps clean the liver, blood, and other vital organs. It improves elimination so that the toxins can be eliminated from the body. Utilizing a cleansing diet and drinking enough purified water are the first steps to starting a new way of life.

I have witnessed over and over again that a customized nutritional protocol speeds the post-addition recovery process. There are thousands of nutritional products available that can help the recovering person. Some are very useful. Some are a waste of money and can actually cause other types of problems if used. Take the time and find someone who really knows the field of nutrition as it relates to recovery to help you. The money you spend on high quality food and nutritional produce will probably be less than you spent on alcohol or other addictive habits. If you add in the additional cost of lost potential from using alcohol, you will probably save money in the long run!

After you have restored a proper diet to your life, it is probably wise to add some specific cleansing or fasting detoxes to your recovery.

Anyone can fast for one day or do a three-day vegetable juice cleanse, but if you really want to feel dramatically better it will require some more advanced cleansing protocols. Again it is important to find someone to help you. Cleansing reactions can vary extensively, and a plan that worked for a friend or that you found on the internet may not be right for you; it may actually hinder your recovery process.

Exercise and rest are also important, not just for the cleansing and strengthening benefits, but for the improvement in mood that is created by the beneficial neurotransmitters released while exercising. As a general rule start slow and do some activity that you find enjoyable. Exercise and fitness is a lifelong goal so it should be fun and work into your time schedule.

People who stop using substances tend to have poor quality sleep. They either cannot fall asleep or they cannot stay asleep. These sleep patterns usually return to normal after about 90 days, though 90 days without sleep can feel like a lifetime.

It may seem confusing to replace one substance for another but herbal and nutritional sleep products can be useful during this period. You need to remember that nutritional products are not drugs and they act like food in our system. These can really make recovery much easier. Diet and exercise also help. It all works together once you make a decision to improve your life by stopping the use of toxic substances. For example, when you sleep better you can think more clearly and have more energy to exercise.

Mental Recovery

Simplifying your day-to-day life enhances mental recovery. Make your life as flexible as possible. Do not take on any nonessential tasks; keep things simple. You are going through a tough period of growth, so remember to be kind to yourself and take it easy. If need be take some time away from work, and rest frequently.

People who are mentally stressed get "locked up" inside their heads. You need to find a way to break free of your mental tendency to have "washing-machine-brain," where you think the same thoughts over and over. Whether the reoccurring thoughts are related to anger, fear, or resentment, you need a way to break the cycle and start a healthier pattern of living in the present moment.

Mindfulness meditation is an easy way to do this. Simply focus on what is in front of you *now*. When your mind wanders (and it most certainly will) bring your attention back to the present moment.

Doing this over and over again is difficult, but over time it becomes a habit. I can tell you with certainty that there is rarely any fear in the present moment. If the mind drifts back into the past or forward into the future, you will without a doubt find fear there also.

Stay in the present moment. This is a fantastic way to start living a new healthier life. Most addictive stress is emotional, and if you've been handling this stress by using drugs or alcohol, you must have a way to set yourself free mentally. In addition to using the above method of staying in the present moment, you will need to develop the ability to see your emotions in an impersonal, non-attached way. This is an effective means to give yourself some distance between you and the feelings you are experiencing.

For example, if you wake up in the middle of the night worried about not having enough money to pay your bills, or resentful at what someone did to you, try this exercise:

> Quiet yourself as best you can at that moment. Sit up on the edge of your bed, and take three deep breaths. Visualize yourself *looking out of your eyes* from the center of your head. This is not like how you normally see with your eyes; you are visualizing yourself looking *through* your eyes like two telescopes. Look at the fearful or resentful situation as if it is in the distance a mile away. Take the same technique and look at other *positive* aspects of your life. Look at 10 or 20 good and wonderful things happening in your life right now.

This simple exercise is a very powerful way to change your perspective and give yourself some emotional objectivity.

By doing this exercise, you start to see your problems as something outside of yourself. You gain perspective. Continue to breathe slowly, until the fear or other strong emotion leaves you. Now sit quietly for a few minutes. Often during this quiet time that follows, an inspirational idea or solution will appear to you. If that happens it may be the start of a way to permanently eliminate this problem in your life. If it seems wise, put this new idea into action.

Spiritual Recovery

For those whose addiction can be identified as being on the spiritual level, you will need some extra help. The desire to feel full and complete is normal, but when we attempt to fill that need on our own, or with the help of drugs and alcohol, we will develop a painful addictive pattern.

For permanent recovery to take place you will need to incorporate an effective spiritual solution. This is not to say that your solution must be religious, though many people do find help in religions. The solution must put you in a personal relationship with a force or intelligence greater than yourself. This spiritual relationship will need to be strong, real, and practical if it is going to help you change your life.

Spiritual practice will be the most fascinating part of your life. It will help alleviate your fears and give you moment-to-moment help in any situation. This relationship is as real as the ground you are standing on right now.

12-step programs are one option. The purpose of these organizations is to help the sufferer find and tap into a power greater than themselves and to have spiritual awakening as a result of an ongoing relationship with that power. Many people utilizing 12-step programs recover and go on to live healthy, functioning lives. In addition to the spiritual guidelines laid out in 12-step programs, these groups provide a tremendous amount of social support and practical guidance to those who attend regularly. For anyone who acknowledges an addictive problem and is willing to seek help, I highly recommend that you attend several different meetings to find one that resonates with you and for you. The general guideline is to attend 90 meetings in your first 90 days of recovery. If you are willing to keep an open mind and be honest, I assure you that you will learn something.

For those who do not find 12-step programs to be a good fit, there are some other options. Recommitting to a church where you feel comfortable and that supports your recovery can be very beneficial. Spiritual retreats and workshops may help. Daily mediation and devotional practices are also uplifting. Many people channel their recovery efforts into various forms of yoga.

I have met many people who have reversed their dysfunctional lives by applying spiritual principles. This can be regular prayer, scripture reading, church attendance, meditation, or selfless service to others.

Some of the mandatory requirements of all spiritual growth is to be honest and disciplined when it comes to yourself, and very gentle and forgiving when it comes to other people. You need to focus on your own growth. Let God work in other people's lives in the way He sees fit. It is none or our business what other people do. We each have enough personal areas in which we can improve to stay very busy!

The observation I made at the top of this chapter, "You cannot stop a bad habit; you can only replace it with a better one," is very true. For those of you who are in, or have dealt with, an addictive relationship, it is critical to find positive activities that rechannel the time and energy you spent on addictive behavior. Find something you love to do that is healthy and does not create new addictive patterns, and do it.

It will need to be some activity that is exciting, enjoyable, and appropriate, given your current emotional, physical, and financial situation. Stay busy doing "good things" for yourself and other people. This is the surest way to find value in your life and to stop the repeating cycle of addiction.

A general rule is that if you ever question whether your addictive behavior is affecting your relationship, it already is. The importance of being free of addictions cannot be overemphasized if you want a healthy relationship with another person. The primary relationship every addict has is always with the substance or behavior they are addicted to. Because addiction causes an obsessive preoccupation to these substances, all other relationships become secondary.

When you are free of addictions you have a consistency in your moods, feelings, and behaviors. This stability is the foundation on which you can build a solid and happy life.

When you are clean and clear you have more energy and focus to channel into your relationships with other people. You are more receptive to other peoples' needs, and you are able to respond in a reliable and loving way.

Key Ideas to Remember

- If you're having a relationship with alcohol, you cannot have a healthy relationship with another person.
- Stop using drugs and alcohol to deal with life.
- Change your diet to one that optimizes your health.
- Cleanse your body of all toxins.
- Simplify your life.
- Develop the practice of staying in the present moment.
- Adopt a disciplined spiritual practice that encourages your growth and minimizes your self-centered focus on you and your problems.

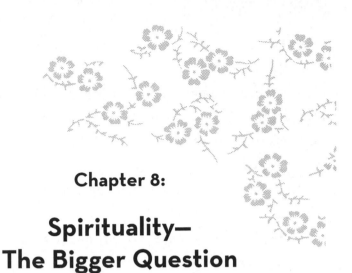

Chapter 8:

Spirituality—
The Bigger Question

"We are all looking for ways to keep the ground
from shifting under our feet."
-Anthony Chadwell

The Issues

Many people may not see the purpose of having a chapter on spirituality in a book about relationships, but if we are going to talk about a holistic approach to relationships, it must include looking at the importance of spirituality and how spirituality affects the quality of our interactions with other people.

I realize that spirituality is a very broad topic, with as many differing views about it as there are people reading this chapter. Some of us were born into families with very clear religious beliefs. We may have attended church regularly and may have participated in various rituals and ceremonies. Others may have grown up in a home where the idea of anything spiritual or religious was never mentioned. No matter what your background the information in this chapter can be helpful to you to create more balance in your relationships and your life

I was born, baptized, and confirmed in the Lutheran church. I always felt a longing need for God to be more to me than an hour-a-week experience. Many find weekly church attendance uplifting and fulfilling, but it was not enough for me. I needed to somehow learn how to carry that spiritual connection throughout the entire week.

I knew I did not create myself, and I certainly had no idea how I happened to end up on planet earth. I always felt there was something "more" to this life. I wanted to be able to tap into this intuitive knowledge, develop and hold onto that awareness. I began to explore additional opportunities for spiritual development when I started taking yoga classes at a young age. This experience was very helpful to me. It introduced me to a different concept of God than I had been aware of prior. I learned how to sit still and meditate from the Eastern philosophies. These aspects of spirituality were not emphasized in my Christian upbringing. I found them to be an important aspect to my feeling closer to God.

When I combined the love and devotion of the Christian tradition with the focused meditation of the Eastern religions, I found I really had a spiritual path that worked for me.

Let me be clear, I am not saying that I have "arrived" when it comes to relationships or spirituality. What I do know is that I have started to grow spiritually. My relationship with God has developed to a level at which I feel pretty peaceful most of the time. As a result of that peacefulness, I am more content. I do not usually look outside of myself for happiness or security, and that is a fantastic feeling. A by-product of this contentment is that I don't need the same things from other people that I used to seek. In the past it was common for me, like many of us, to look to other people for approval, distraction, or entertainment.

I love people, enjoy their company, and find their lives interesting. I just don't *need* as much from them as before. Ironically, without the pressure that the "needing" causes, people become more relaxed. The relaxation they feel becomes "the something" of which they want more. Spiritual awareness in this context becomes self-perpetuating.

Living a life supported by spiritual beliefs and values adds a solid basis from which you can construct all of your other relationships. It has been my experience that until you feel at ease with yourself, comfortable in the world and your own place in it, you will continue looking for escape outside of yourself.

The Root Cause

This book has given many examples of how people use relationships to try to *look outside of themselves* for the peace, contentment and the joy they seek. An infinite set of possibilities exists when it comes to relationships. The relationships in which you are involved may never be perfect, but those are the relationships you have. Imperfection, in fact, is a natural law in this world.

A blossoming spirituality allows you to live comfortably with the imperfections life presents along the way; it provides a much broader context for understanding your challenges as you navigate your life here on earth.

Carol

Carol came to see me for cranial therapy after a series of stressful situations had taken place. She was generally happy with her life, but she had a nagging feeling she could feel better. Her sleep was poor, and she felt fatigued. Along with cranial sacral therapy, she started on a nutritional protocol. After a few weeks her energy improved. She felt less agitated, yet she still had a longing in her heart to feel more of a purpose to her life than she was currently experiencing.

When I asked her about her spiritual beliefs, she explained that she was raised a Catholic but had drifted away from the church after she left for college and started studying science. She experienced a spiritual conflict, unable to reconcile the differences between these two seemingly divergent points of view.

When I asked her if she'd ever reconsidered going back and investigating the church as an open-minded and intelligent adult, she sheepishly acknowledged that she had not.

We spent some time talking about the nature of being human, the difficulties of life, and the desire to find a paradigm of understanding reality that allowed her to feel safe and have a purpose. Carol said she would consider investigating her old church and left the office with a curious expression on her face. I did not know it at that moment, but Carol had had an epiphany during the session.

A month later Carol came back into the office. I noticed a lightness and ease around her that had not been there before. She explained that she had indeed gone back to the Catholic church, had spoken to a priest about her frustration, about the circumstances that initiated her leaving the church some 20 years before.

Carol told me that where she had felt judged and shamed as a child, she now felt welcomed and supported. An institution that had intimidated her in her youth now seemed it might provide at least part of the answer she was seeking: an explanation of the purpose for her life and a spiritual focal point that gave her life some perspective.

Carol was unique because of her humility and willingness to reinvestigate an organization she had "written off" years before. She also brought a great amount of humility, openness, and willingness to her search for clarity and purpose. She told me something I had heard many times before from other people: she was now grateful for her parents "dragging" her to church when she was young. Even though she resented it at the time and rebelled against it later, the "seed had been planted."

Blane

Most people who enter a 12-step program have hit some type of "bottom." Hitting bottom in our lives can be a pivotal point in becoming willing to accept spiritual help for a situation that has no other solution.

Blane's story is no different. After abusing drugs and alcohol for 12 years, Blain's life was a chaotic mess. He was in trouble with the law, the IRS, his ex-wife, and his employer. His life was in so much turmoil, he felt he had no choice but to "give up." In that place of defeat he had one of those "moments-of-clarity" that allowed him to see his life for exactly what it was: a complete failure.

Blain said a simple prayer, "God help me." There were no conditions attached to that request for help; he just yielded his will to God's will, and he yielded it sincerely at his core. As is common to recovering people, his life took on miraculous dimensions. He was able to stop drinking and using drugs for the first time in his adult life. More importantly, he was able to "stay stopped." Why? He had had a spiritual experience—much like the mystics of the past have written about. This transformation expanded into other areas of Blane's life. He started to see his former behaviors with much more clarity, and was able to acknowledge that his ex-wife had actually been right about certain things, and he had been wrong. Humility crept into his life, and he started helping other people in recovery. Becoming genuinely interested in other people's welfare, beyond his own immediate needs, added an aspect of gratitude he had been unable to tap before. He eventually reconciled with his wife!

As Blane's perspective of the world around him widened, he began feeling a genuine gratitude for his job, realizing that (especially in these hard times) it was a luxury to have a job in the first place. He began to approach his work with more of that gratitude he was feeling, consciously giving more than his "fair share" and putting the company's interests first. He was soon promoted, and his coworkers thought highly of him. Blane began to have the will, energy, and clarity to get his life a little more in order every day.

He made an arrangement with the IRS and paid off the money he owed in back taxes. In addition his health improved, and he began to sleep well at night.

All of these changes happened in a very short timeframe. It seemed like a miracle, and to Blane it was. He had given his will over to a higher power for guidance, and that higher power provided. Blane is convinced that God intervened. God had solved his problems in a way that Blane could not understand, or could not have accomplished on his own effort alone. He is a new man. His openness to letting true spirituality permeate his being was rewarded with blessings he could not have predicted.

The Solution

In whatever circumstances you find yourself, make the best of them now. Be the best person you are capable of being in body, mind, and spirit. Today. Not tomorrow or next week. Some wise Greek person knew what he was saying when he coined the term "carpe diem," meaning "seize the day."

If you are overweight or unhealthy, channel your energy (today) into improving your health, not with the secret intention of finding someone, but just to become the best person you possible can be. A healthy and fit body is simply a better vehicle from which to enjoy life.

If some of the emotional issues covered in this book are active in your life, put effort into cleaning up these areas of limitation. This book is full of practical suggestions to help you improve in those areas. If your problems are serious, make the effort to seek professional assistance.

Notice your spiritual life. If it is lacking or non-existent, you will find no better area to devote your time and energy than to develop that important aspect of your humanity.

If you have some idea what your spiritual "path" is, get to work! *Life here on earth is much shorter than we believe*; don't waste time complaining about problems of "romance and finance." These types of problems are endless; sometimes the only option we have is to step outside of our current circumstances and see our lives in the greater context. With practice we learn that this option is actually one that we can apply on a regular basis in our lives to "check in" with ourselves, to be sure the choices we're making are leading to the fulfillment of what we've determined our ultimate life purpose to be. This checking in will enrich everything we create and do.

We are human. Humans make mistakes, and our lives are temporary, yet we have a great deal of control over how we accept our situations. You live for some number of years, and then you move on to some other, I believe, greater experience.

When you can hold onto this "larger" perspective, it is astounding how your problems fade in significance. Perspective is a good thing. Practice broadening it outside of yourself regularly.

If you have no idea where to start when it comes to a spiritual ideal, that is fine too. Often your higher power will reveal the first step you need to take in quiet whispers that you must be listening carefully to hear. None of us gets to see the end result at the beginning of any journey. If your first step is to buy a book, attend a seminar, go to a church or meditation, do that. You are responsible for taking the action; God is responsible for the outcome.

What I hope to have accomplished in this chapter is to illustrate that looking for comfort outside of ourselves is only a temporary solution. Some options may seem to work for a while, but in the end, the external approach to seeking happiness is not fulfilling. The longings many of us feel inside our hearts can never be fully (or often, even partially) satisfied with material objects or distractions.

Some of the benefits of living a spiritually-centered life include

- More peace
- More tolerance of other people and situations
- More intuition concerning decisions and problem solving
- More love and compassion
- More charity and benevolence

Focusing on problems is easy, because that is what much of life presents to us. In our culture most of our pain is caused by frustrated ego desires. A spiritual perspective refocuses your life and lets you live in peace with yourself, with other people, and with the world at large.

Key Ideas to Remember

- A solid spiritual life helps strengthen all of your other relationships.
- Each of us has the potential to find our own spiritual path. It is my belief that all humans have been hardwired to do so.
- Start by taking the first indicated step. The next step will appear, when you trust in it, and when it is time.
- Be consistent in your spiritual practice.
- Share your experience with others.

Conclusion

Put simply, it *is* possible to get over past hurts and dysfunctional patterns. Doing the work is necessary, but it is not as difficult as you may believe. The practical suggestions given in this book provide you with tangible help to clarify what change is needed. The result of doing this work is that you will handle relationship situations in healthier ways and feel better about yourself in the process. You will attract people into your life with this higher level of consciousness.

This kind of growth is self-perpetuating. Once you experience the sweetness this change brings into your life, you will want more and more of it. When you make conscious improvement in even one aspect of your life, it will improve all of your relationships. For example, trusting yourself to make good decisions, you'll see how that experience transfers to other areas such as work and health.

This process is a fascinating evolution, one you will not want to miss. Use this book as a great place to start to gain more clarity for your own life. Then, by example, share that clarity and the fresh hope it brings with those you come in contact with throughout your day. This is one of the greatest rewards of higher consciousness.

Many blessings to you and yours,
Anthony Chadwell

Resources

For more information, or to contact Anthony Chadwell,
please visit our website at:
www.chadwellmethod.com